IT Capability Maturity Framework™ (IT-CMF™)

A Management Guide

Other publications by Van Haren Publishing

Van Haren Publishing (VHP) specializes in titles on Best Practices, methods and standards within four domains:
- IT and IT Management
- Architecture (Enterprise and IT)
- Business Management and
- Project Management

Van Haren Publishing offers a wide collection of whitepapers, templates, free e-books, trainer materials etc. in the **Van Haren Publishing Knowledge Base**: www.vanharen.net for more details.

Van Haren Publishing is also publishing on behalf of leading organizations and companies: ASLBiSL Foundation, BRMI, CA, Centre Henri Tudor, Gaming Works, IACCM, IAOP, Innovation Value Institute, IPMA-NL, ITSqc, NAF, KNVI, PMI-NL, PON, The Open Group, The SOX Institute.

Topics are (per domain):

IT and IT Management	Enterprise Architecture	Project Management
ABC of ICT	ArchiMate®	A4-Projectmanagement
ASL®	GEA®	DSDM/Atern
CATS CM®	Novius Architectuur Methode	ICB / NCB
CMMI®	TOGAF®	ISO 21500
COBIT®		MINCE®
e-CF	**Business Management**	M_o_R®
ISO 20000	*BABOK® Guide*	MSP®
ISO 27001/27002	BiSL® and BiSL® Next	P3O®
ISPL	BRMBOK™	*PMBOK® Guide*
IT4IT®	BTF	PRINCE2®
IT-CMF™	EFQM	
IT Service CMM	eSCM	
ITIL®	IACCM	
MOF	ISA-95	
MSF	ISO 9000/9001	
SABSA	OPBOK	
SAF	SixSigma	
SIAM	SOX	
	SqEME®	

For the latest information on VHP publications, visit our website: www.vanharen.net.

IT Capability Maturity Framework™ (IT-CMF™)

A Management Guide

Edited by:
Martin Curley, Jim Kenneally,
Marian Carcary, Declan Kavanagh

Contributing Authors:
Martin Curley, Jim Kenneally, Marian Carcary, Eileen Doherty, Gerard Conway,
Catherine Crowley, Conor O'Brien, Clare Thornley, Sinéad Murnane,
Louise Veling, Declan Kavanagh, Michael Hanley, Martin Delaney, Anna Browne

INNOVATION™
VALUE
INSTITUTE

Maynooth University
National University
of Ireland Maynooth

TECHNOLOGY CENTRE
ENTERPRISE IRELAND
IDA IRELAND SUPPORTED

Title:	IT-CMF – A Management Guide: Based on the IT Capability Maturity Framework™ (IT-CMF™) 2nd edition
Edited by:	Prof. Martin Curley, Jim Kenneally, Dr Marian Carcary, Declan Kavanagh
Contributing authors:	Prof. Martin Curley, Jim Kenneally, Dr Marian Carcary, Dr Eileen Doherty, Gerard Conway, Catherine Crowley, Conor O'Brien, Dr Clare Thornley, Sinéad Murnane, Louise Veling, Declan Kavanagh, Michael Hanley, Martin Delaney, Anna Browne
Publisher:	Van Haren Publishing, Zaltbommel, www.vanharen.net
Editorial & design consultants:	Rédacteurs Limited, www.redact.ie
Design & layout:	Coco Bookmedia, Amersfoort – NL
NUR code:	981 / 123
ISBN hard copy:	978 94 018 0196 6
ISBN eBook (pdf):	978 94 018 0197 3
Edition:	First edition, first impression, August 2017
Copyright:	© Innovation Value Institute (a research centre of Maynooth University) / Van Haren Publishing, 2017

Preface

The IT Capability Maturity Framework (IT-CMF) is a framework specifically created to help organizations derive real, measurable business value from IT. This management guide helps IT leaders and professionals at all levels to understand IT-CMF and begin to apply it in their day-to-day improvement activities.

IT-CMF was developed to help organizations meet the challenges they face in managing the array of discrete but independent IT management disciplines focused on the generation of IT-enabled agility, innovation, and value. It is underpinned by proven concepts and principles that provide organizations with a coherent guide to developing IT capabilities that can help them innovate, grow, and prosper. With the advent of Social, Mobile, Analytics, Cloud and the Internet of Things (SMACIT), digital business transformation is top of the agenda for most organizations, and IT-CMF provides a body of knowledge, tools, techniques, and guidance for IT leaders and professionals to support their organization's digital agenda.

This management guide is derived from the comprehensive work of the Innovation Value Institute, as encapsulated in *IT Capability Maturity Framework: The Body of Knowledge Guide* (2nd edition, 2016).

What's in this book

This management guide is intended as a quick reference guide for those who wish to understand the essentials of IT-CMF or those who are implementing IT-CMF to manage IT value and IT-enabled innovation within their organizations. This book has four parts:

▶ Part A describes the background to IT-CMF, how it was developed and what makes it valuable as a framework for IT management. This covers the core concepts that underpin IT-CMF, its capability architecture, and an overview of how to use IT-CMF to manage capability improvement – including a brief description of each of the four phases in the Capability Improvement Programme (CIP).
▶ Part B presents high-level summaries of IT-CMF's four Macro-Capabilities and their thirty-six constituent Critical Capabilities.
▶ Part C outlines the next steps that someone embarking on an IT-CMF initiative might take – for example, to assess and benchmark their current capabilities and to launch an improvement programme.

▶ Part D (appendices) summarises the supports that the Innovation Value Institute makes available to those who are embarking on an IT-CMF initiative – these include assessment and training options, a summary of capability performance indicators for each Critical Capability, and descriptions of key artefacts (tools and templates).

About the Innovation Value Institute™

The Innovation Value Institute (IVI) was established in 2006 as a not-for-profit multidisciplinary research and education institute within Maynooth University, Ireland. It was co-founded by Intel Corporation and the university with the objective of creating an international consortium of companies and public sector organizations to build on work already carried out in Intel and create an international standard for the management of IT.

As well as the consortium's commitment of funding and in-kind resources, Enterprise Ireland and IDA Ireland, through the Technology Centre programme, support IVI's research agenda to focus on the creation and accumulation of knowledge and best-available practices in the management of IT.

IVI supports and is supported by an international membership consortium of industry, academia, and public sector organizations who collaborate to deepen their understanding and develop their ability to manage their IT functions and realize the value of IT for their organizations. The consortium currently includes over 100 members, including many of the world's largest and most prestigious enterprises. Collaboration with the consortium members is a key part of IVI's research and development process.

The Origins of IT-CMF™

In 2000, when Intel Corporation embarked on a programme of transformation of its IT function, they found that there was no comprehensive, integrated, CIO-level framework available. Over the following years, they developed a maturity framework approach that proved to be highly successful. That approach, and the lessons learned from their experience of applying it, were captured in Professor Martin Curley's book, *Managing IT for Business Value*. When IVI was established in 2006, the Institute adopted the maturity framework from Intel Corporation, and continued to further develop and refine it. Since then, IVI has substantially enhanced and extended the framework with further research and feedback from users, to make it relevant to IT leaders and professionals in any industry (public or private) who need to manage key IT capabilities to improve agility, innovation, and value.

Acknowledgements

Development of IT-CMF is made possible by the many individuals from organizations spanning industry, government, and academia throughout the world, who donated their time to add richness, relevance, and rigour to the body of knowledge. The Innovation Value Institute (IVI) is grateful to these people and their organizations.

Contents

Managing the IT Capability

Managing IT for Business Value

C. GOING FORWARD WITH IT-CMF

D. APPENDICES

A. Introduction

The Management of IT Challenge

The rapid developments in information technology (IT) present a challenge for people working in all organizations – large and small, public and private. IT-enabled change and innovation are increasingly critical for organizations' continued viability, but many people struggle to use IT effectively in ways that optimize its value across organizations.

In short, there is a lack of tools and resources to manage *how* organizations can get the best out of IT. As many as half of all large-scale technology deployments risk failure – not because they don't provide imaginative solutions to real-world issues or because they lack inherent value, but rather because they are deployed without an appropriate IT management structure. And with estimated annual worldwide IT spending at around US$2 trillion, such failures represent a very significant financial loss, not to speak of the lost opportunities to deliver value and innovation.

Organizations must deploy and use IT effectively to remain relevant in an increasingly digital economy, and they must continually innovate and differentiate themselves to keep pace and gain competitive advantage, particularly in the face of the transformation that is arriving with SMACIT (Social, Mobile, Analytics, Cloud and the Internet of Things). IT on its own does not create business success – only an effective IT capability that delivers a steady stream of IT-enabled changes and innovations can provide sustainable competitive advantage.

What Is IT-CMF?

IT-CMF is an integrated management framework and set of tools for designing, deploying, and operating information systems to deliver sustainable business value and innovation.

It incorporates a comprehensive body of knowledge that covers thirty-six critical IT management capabilities that enable practitioners to measure the *maturity* of different levels of management efficiency and effectiveness. It also has a portfolio of certified training and accreditation, tools and templates, and a comprehensive Capability Improvement Programme that enables practitioners to professionalize their entire approach to IT management.

IT-CMF is explicitly designed to cover the full range of IT capabilities that are required to deliver agility, innovation, and value for the organization. And it is also flexibly designed to allow new capabilities to be captured, represented, and integrated as they emerge.

Organizations that are good at managing their IT capabilities perform better as businesses, but many organizations struggle to manage their IT capabilities in a coherent, systematic, or focused way. One of the fundamental values of IT-CMF is that it enables decision-makers to identify and develop the particular IT capabilities they need in order to deliver agility, innovation, and value to their organization.

The Unique and Comprehensive Scope of IT-CMF

Of course, there are other IT management tools that cover individual domains, that specialize in particular niche areas, or that focus on certain known IT management deficits. The fact that there are so many tools, however, makes it even more difficult for organizations to choose the ones that are appropriate to their needs and then to integrate them effectively. IT-CMF, by contrast, offers comprehensive coverage of the full range of defined IT-related capabilities, and is flexible enough to accommodate new capabilities as they emerge. It also has the very considerable advantage of offering a clear and common language for defining levels of maturity and for identifying ways in which deficits might be addressed.

IT-CMF aims for comprehensive coverage of the components (*Critical Capabilities*) needed by those responsible for managing the IT function in an organization. It leverages the concept of dynamic capabilities that can be reconfigured as required to meet changing circumstances and strategies. It provides a portfolio of options from which IT leaders and professionals can design an improvement programme that is uniquely suited to their particular IT capability needs and their business environment.

IT-CMF builds on the maturity model conceptualization adopted by the Software Engineering Institute for the Software CMM model, but as well as focusing on process and capability maturity, IT-CMF also focuses on outcome maturity – that is, on the specific business outcomes expected at different levels of capability maturity.

The Innovation Value Institute™

IT-CMF was developed by the Innovation Value Institute (IVI), a not-for-profit, multidisciplinary research and education institute established in 2006. The Institute was co-founded by Intel Corporation and Maynooth University with the objective of creating an international consortium of companies and public sector organizations to build on work already carried out in Intel and create an international standard for the management of IT.

As well as the consortium's commitment of funding and in-kind resources, Enterprise Ireland and IDA Ireland, through the Technology Centre programme, support IVI's research agenda with its focus on the creation and accumulation of knowledge and best-available practices in the management of IT.

The consortium currently includes over 100 members, including many of the world's largest and most prestigious enterprises. Collaboration with the consortium members is a key part of IVI's research and development process (Open Innovation 2.0).

What IT-CMF Provides

IT-CMF provides the basis for systematically and continually improving the performance of the IT function in an organization, and for measuring progress and value delivered. It enables organizations to devise more robust strategies, make better-informed decisions, and consistently deliver increased levels of agility, innovation, and value.

IT-CMF offers:

▶ A holistic business-led approach that enables performance across the IT function to be managed consistently and comprehensively.

▶ Support for the development of enduring IT capabilities with a primary focus on achieving business agility, innovation, and value.

▶ A platform and a common language for exchanging information between diverse stakeholders, enabling them to set goals, take action, and evaluate improvements.

▶ An umbrella framework that complements other frameworks already in use in the organization to drive cohesive performance improvement.

IT-CMF is currently used by hundreds of organizations worldwide, and is fast becoming the de facto standard for the management of IT in large organizations.

Core Concepts of IT-CMF

This section outlines the core principles and philosophy underpinning IT-CMF. A good understanding of these concepts will help the reader to derive optimum benefit from the remaining chapters of this book, and to see how IT-CMF improves management of IT for better agility, innovation, and value.

What is a Capability?

A capability is the *quality of being capable*, to have the capacity or ability to do something, to achieve pre-determined goals and objectives. Collectively, capabilities coordinate the activities of individuals and groups – linking individual actions into seamless chains of actions, leading to repeatable patterns of interaction that become more efficient and effective as they are practised and internalized. An organizational capability refers to an organization's ability to *'perform a set of co-ordinated tasks, utilizing organizational resources, for the purposes of achieving a particular end result'* [1].

Capabilities must work in a consistent manner. Having a capability means that the organization can perform an activity repeatedly and reliably. Organizations build their capabilities progressively in a cyclical process of trial, feedback, learning, and evolution. Organizations must be able to realign their resources in response to changes in strategy or the environment in which they operate. They must be able to embrace change, quickly innovating and reconfiguring resources to capture and exploit new, unforeseen opportunities. This is often referred to as having 'dynamic' capabilities. IT-CMF facilitates this flexibility and responsiveness, and enables an organization to purposefully create, extend, or modify its resource base to address rapidly changing circumstances [2].

Dynamic capabilities include the ability to search, explore, acquire, assimilate, and apply knowledge about resources and opportunities, and about how resources can be configured to exploit opportunities. Organizations with such capabilities have greater intensity of organizational learning, and are able to leverage feedback cycles more effectively, and thereby continually build stronger capabilities.

IT Capabilities

An organization's ability to orchestrate IT-based resources to create desired outcomes is a product of its IT capabilities. In IT-CMF, an IT capability is *the ability to mobilize and deploy (that is, integrate, reconfigure, acquire, and release) IT-based resources to effect a desired end, often in combination with other resources and capabilities* (adapted [3]). Resources, in this context, can be either tangible (including financial, physical/infrastructural, human) or intangible (including software, data, intellectual property, branding, culture).

Relationships between Capabilities, Competences, and Processes

Business processes are sequences of actions that organizations engage in to accomplish specific tasks. They represent how an organization's resources are exploited, and can be thought of as the routines or activities that an organization develops to get something done [4][5]. Business processes require the competences (knowledge, skills, and experience) of individual employees and groups for their effective execution. In turn, business processes help individual employees and groups develop competence in particular ways of working [6]. Processes and competences are thus mutually dependent and reinforcing.

Effective and efficient processes are critical for business operations, but they must be regularly evaluated and where necessary modified to ensure that they continue to meet the organization's ongoing requirements and to deliver sustainable business value. Capability management provides the vital link between the business's strategy and environment and its business processes. It gives the organization *the ability to create patterns of learning and adjustment and to establish and maintain synergetic relationships between competences (people), processes (routines), and resources (assets) to accomplish a desired end*.

Business Value

The term 'business value' is commonly used to refer to the overall health of an organization, and includes both economic value and other forms that cannot always be measured in monetary terms. IT-CMF reflects a narrower focus on the concept and defines business value from its perspective as *the contribution that IT-based resources and capabilities make to helping an organization achieve its objectives* [7]. Those objectives may be internal or external to the IT function. IT's greatest potential, however, lies in business enablement across the wider organization – that is, the organization's IT capability plays an important role in developing other business capabilities [3]. In having an effective IT capability, the organization is enabled to strategically mobilize and deploy (integrate, reconfigure, acquire, and release) its various resources to achieve specific goals and objectives, often in combination with other capabilities and resources, and it is only through this process that business value is delivered. As outlined above, resources in this context can include, for example, financial, physical/ infrastructural, human, data, intellectual property, branding, and culture, and depending on the organization's context, these resources will likely be coordinated and integrated in different ways. Hence, while all organizations have an IT capability, the resource configurations that underpin this capability will differ, thereby determining whether the organization's IT capability is weak or strong [8]. IT-CMF helps organizations to continually enhance their capabilities to ensure that the underpinning resource (re)configurations are always aligned in support of business strategy and in response to environmental forces.

Maturity

Maturity frameworks are conceptual models that outline anticipated, typical, logical, and desired evolution paths towards desired end-states [9], where maturity is an evolutionary progress in the demonstration of a specific ability or in the accomplishment of a target [10]. Maturity-based approaches for managing IT have been widely adopted – for example, the Software Engineering Institute's (SEI) Capability Maturity Model Integration (CMMI) is extensively used in the domain of software quality [11][12].

For each of the capabilities in the framework, IT-CMF defines five maturity levels, each of which identifies a different level of efficiency and effectiveness. This facilitates a modular, systematic, and incremental approach to capability improvement, by helping organizations to gauge how advanced they are in each area of activity, and identifying the actions they can take to improve over time.

While the definition of maturity levels is specific to each capability, the broad common characteristics of the five maturity levels, in terms of approaches, scope, and outcomes, are as shown in Table 1.

Maturity levels are additive in that each lower level provides the foundation for the next level, and capabilities are progressively enhanced from one level to the next. It can thus be unwise (and may not be possible) to skip levels – for example, to attempt to progress from level 1 directly to level 5. With proper planning, however, progress through the levels can be accelerated.

TABLE 1: GENERAL MATURITY LEVEL HEURISTICS

Level	Approaches Quality of routines / practices or activities	Scope Breadth of coverage / focus	Outcomes Predictability between actions and consequences
1 – Initial	Approaches are inadequate and unstable.	Scope is fragmented and incoherent.	Repeatable outcomes are rare.
2 – Basic	Approaches are defined, but inconsistencies remain.	Scope is limited to a partial area of a business function or domain area; deficiencies remain.	Repeatable outcomes are achieved occasionally.
3 – Intermediate	Approaches are standardized, inconsistencies are addressed.	Scope expands to cover a business function (typically IT) or domain area.	Repeatable outcomes are often achieved.
4 – Advanced	Approaches can systematically flex for innovative adaptations.	Scope covers the end-to-end organization / neighbouring domain areas.	Repeatable outcomes are very often achieved.
5 – Optimizing	Approaches demonstrate world-class attributes.	Scope extends beyond the borders of the organization / neighbouring domains.	Repeatable outcomes are virtually always achieved.

The Architecture of IT-CMF

IT-CMF is structured, at the highest level, around four *Macro-Capabilities*, each of which embraces a number of *Critical Capabilities* that can contribute to agility, innovation, and value. Each Critical Capability in turn is made up of a number of *Capability Building Blocks*.

4 Macro-Capabilities

    → **36 Critical Capabilities**

        → **315 Capability Building Blocks**

IT-CMF defines the different *maturity levels* for each Capability Building Block, and provides *evaluation questions* to assess their current 'as is' state. For each Capability Building Block, IT-CMF provides a series of representative practices to drive maturity, along with the outcomes that can be expected from implementing them, and the metrics that can be applied to monitor progress (*Practices-Outcomes-Metrics*, or *POMs*).

The framework also looks at typical *challenges* that the organization might face in attempting to develop maturity in each capability, and suggests *actions to overcome* them. And it identifies additional *management artefacts* and *capability performance indicators (CPIs)* that can be used in progressing towards a target 'to be' maturity state.

Macro-Capabilities

At the highest level, IT-CMF is structured around four key strategic areas, or Macro-Capabilities, for the management of IT:

1. Managing IT like a business.
2. Managing the IT budget.
3. Managing the IT capability.
4. Managing IT for business value.

The effective management of technology within an organization focuses on these four Macro-Capabilities, all of which should be aligned with the overall business strategy, the business environment within which the organization operates, and the IT posture of the organization – i.e. the organization's attitude towards the use of IT.

---

1. Managing IT like a Business

To optimize the contribution of technology to the organization as a whole, the IT function needs to be managed using professional business practices. This involves shifting the focus away from technology as an end in itself towards the customers and the business problems to which IT can provide solutions. The **Managing IT Like a Business** Macro-Capability provides a structure within which the IT function can be repositioned from a cost centre to a value centre.

---

2. Managing the IT Budget

There are many challenges associated with managing the IT budget, including, for example, unplanned cost escalation, the cost of maintaining legacy systems, and management reluctance to invest strategically in new technologies. The **Managing the IT Budget** Macro-Capability looks at the practices and tools that can be used to establish and control a sustainable economic funding model for IT services and solutions.

---

3. Managing the IT Capability

The IT function was traditionally seen as the provider of one-off IT services and solutions. In order to fulfil its role as the instigator of innovation and continual business improvement however, the IT function has to proactively deliver – and be seen to deliver – a stream of new and improved IT services and solutions. The **Managing the IT Capability** Macro-Capability provides a systematic approach to adopting that role, by effectively and efficiently maintaining existing services and solutions and developing new ones.

---

4. Managing IT for Business Value

Investments in IT must be linked to overall business benefits. This means that the investments should not be viewed simply as technology projects, but as projects that generate business value and innovation across the organization. The **Managing IT for Business Value** Macro-Capability provides a structure within which the IT function provides the rationale for investment in IT and measures the business benefits accruing from it.

Together these four Macro-Capabilities operate in a continuous feedback loop to optimize the way in which IT is managed.

▶ *Managing IT like a Business* sets the direction for the overall IT capability.
▶ In *Managing the IT Budget*, the strategic direction is translated into an IT budget to fuel activities and programmes.
▶ *Managing the IT Capability* is the production engine, where two primary activities are performed: maintaining existing IT solutions and services, and developing new IT solutions and services.
▶ *Managing IT for Business Value* ensures that these activities and programmes deliver value.

Performance is fed back into *Managing IT like a Business*, to validate that the IT budget is being converted effectively into business value. This may result in tactical or strategic adjustments that feed through the cycle again [13] (See Figure 1).

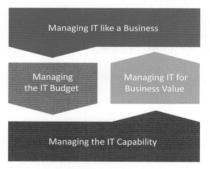

FIGURE 1: IT-CMF's MACRO-CAPABILITIES

The Macro-Capability feedback loop in IT-CMF ensures that the organization continually focuses on the IT capabilities needed to meet the challenges and opportunities presented by the changing business and operating environment. When an organization is planning its capability improvement programme, it is helpful to decide on its strategic objectives in relation to each of the four Macro-Capabilities of IT-CMF, as depicted in Figure 2. This will help to identify the Critical Capabilities that the organization needs to focus on. Other factors that must be taken into account include IT posture, problem context, industry trends, business strategy, business context, and so on.

Critical Capabilities

IT-CMF's four Macro-Capabilities encompass a modular library of 36 Critical Capabilities (See Figure 3). Critical Capabilities are key management domains that need to be considered by an organization when planning and delivering IT-enabled agility, value, and innovation. For each Critical Capability, there are five progressive levels of maturity that describe the state of completeness of an organization's ability to achieve a desired end state or outcome.

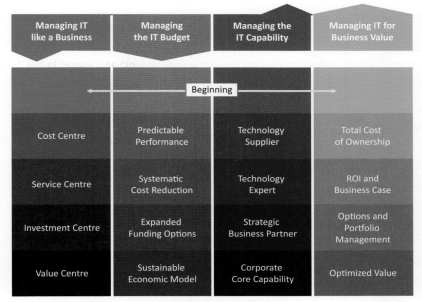

Managing IT like a Business	Managing the IT Budget	Managing the IT Capability	Managing IT for Business Value
Beginning			
Cost Centre	Predictable Performance	Technology Supplier	Total Cost of Ownership
Service Centre	Systematic Cost Reduction	Technology Expert	ROI and Business Case
Investment Centre	Expanded Funding Options	Strategic Business Partner	Options and Portfolio Management
Value Centre	Sustainable Economic Model	Corporate Core Capability	Optimized Value

FIGURE 2: MAJOR STRATEGIES OF IT-CMF'S MACRO-CAPABILITIES

Capability Building Blocks

Capability Building Blocks are the key components of a Critical Capability that enable its goals and objectives to be achieved efficiently and effectively. These are grouped into higher-order logical categories that are particular to each capability. As with Critical Capabilities, there are five progressive levels of maturity for each Capability Building Block.

Additional Capability Components

As well as the three major architectural elements of IT-CMF discussed above and in the following chapters, there are additional capability elements that can help practitioners leverage the full value of the framework. The Capability Maturity Evaluations/Assessments, Practices-Outcomes-Metrics (POMs), and Management Artefacts are outlined in detail in *IT Capability Maturity Framework: The Body of Knowledge Guide* (2nd edition, 2016). A list of all Capability Performance Indicators (CPIs) is included in Appendix 3.

Capability Maturity Evaluations/ Assessments	For each Critical Capability, there is a capability evaluation that is designed to help IT leaders and professionals to determine their organization's current and desired maturity levels in relation to the Critical Capability and its underlying Capability Building Blocks. Each question has associated with it a series of corresponding maturity statements from which the organization selects the one that most closely matches their situation based on survey participants' aggregate responses. These questions and answers can inform improvement planning discussions and help drive improvement across the areas under investigation.

Managing IT like a Business

- (AA) Accounting and Allocation
- (BP) Business Planning
- (BPM) Business Process Management
- (CFP) Capacity Forecasting and Planning
- (DSM) Demand and Supply Management
- (EIM) Enterprise Information Management
- (GIT) Green IT
- (IM) Innovation Management
- (ITG) IT Leadership and Governance
- (ODP) Organization Design and Planning
- (RM) Risk Management
- (SAI) Service Analytics and Intelligence
- (SRC) Sourcing
- (SP) Strategic Planning

Managing the IT Budget

- (BGM) Budget Management
- (BOP) Budget Oversight and Performance Analysis
- (FF) Funding and Financing
- (PPP) Portfolio Planning and Prioritization

Managing the IT Capability

- (CAM) Capability Assessment Management
- (EAM) Enterprise Architecture Management
- (ISM) Information Security Management
- (KAM) Knowledge Asset Management
- (PAM) People Asset Management
- (PDP) Personal Data Protection
- (PPM) Programme and Project Management
- (REM) Relationship Management
- (RDE) Research, Development and Engineering
- (SRP) Service Provisioning
- (SD) Solutions Delivery
- (SUM) Supplier Management
- (TIM) Technical Infrastructure Management
- (UED) User Experience Design
- (UTM) User Training Management

Managing IT for Business Value

- (BAR) Benefits Assessment and Realization
- (PM) Portfolio Management
- (TCO) Total Cost of Ownership

FIGURE 3: IT-CMF'S MACRO-CAPABILITIES AND CRITICAL CAPABILITIES

Practices-Outcomes-Metrics (POMs)	For each Critical Capability, representative *practices* to help stabilize the organization's current maturity or progress to the next level of maturity are described at each maturity level. Each practice is accompanied by an *outcome* that states what benefits might result from following the practice, and one or more *metrics* against which the organization can gauge whether or not it has been successful in its efforts. The practices listed are indicative or representative, and are not exhaustive or mandatory – depending on organizational circumstances, alternative practices may yield the same results.
	IT leaders and professionals choose the POMs that are most appropriate to their organization's maturity circumstances and on which they can expend time, resources, and effort to best effect.
	As with maturity levels, POMs are cumulative, in that lower-level POMs provide the foundation for adopting and succeeding with higher-level POMs.
Capability Performance Indicators (CPIs)	Capability Performance Indicators (CPIs) are those business and operational performance indicators that relate directly to a specific Critical Capability. CPIs are designed to help to make connections between business goals, capability improvement targets, and business outcomes. These are used to help IT leaders and professionals to better understand their organization's progress in relation to expected process outcomes, and to complement day-to-day monitoring, control, and actions.
	The CPIs are grouped into the balanced scorecard segments (financial, process, customer, learning and growth) in order to provide a more holistic view of the target capability improvement. Individuals and teams select a small number of CPIs that are relevant to their improvement priorities.
	A list of all CPIs is included in Appendix 3. Licensed users of IT-CMF can access the full details of all CPIs online via the IVI Digital Platform. CPIs are not included in *IT Capability Maturity Framework: The Body of Knowledge Guide* (2nd edition, 2016).
Management Artefacts	These are artefacts that management might use to develop maturity in Critical Capabilities. They include a range of templates, documents, software applications, and other tools that have the potential to help IT leaders and professionals develop their organization's capability.

The Capability Improvement Programme (CIP)

The Capability Improvement Programme (CIP) is a change methodology and set of tools developed by IVI to support organizations who are implementing IT-CMF. Working with IVI, organizations can use the CIP to identify the Critical Capabilities that deliver the highest value to the business, and then to plan for structured improvement focused on their day-to-day operations.

Each organization undertaking a CIP will have a different business and operational context, and the nature, focus, and level of improvement that they seek will be different. The sophistication and comprehensiveness of IT-CMF accommodates different starting positions and enables organizations to leverage different aspects of the framework.

Who is CIP for?

There are two key types of user who engage in an IT-CMF CIP:

▶ **Practitioners** are those who play a leadership or key facilitating role in addressing the business issue through capability improvement. These include IT leaders and professionals – programme leaders, improvement team leaders, key subject matter experts, and IT-CMF assessors.

▶ **Participants** are those who need to understand the context of the CIP and who participate in activities and tasks related to CIP. They also include senior management and sponsors of CIP.

Training is available in both online e-learning format and class-based format (See Appendix 2 for a list of available training programmes). Formal IVI examinations and certification are available as an option, and many organizations and individuals include certification in support of their quality programmes and career and professional development.

The Four Phases of a CIP

The CIP has four phases, each of which has clearly identified activities, tasks, deliverables, outcomes, and supporting templates directed at the achievement of capability and business goals. Figure 4 presents an overview of the CIP.

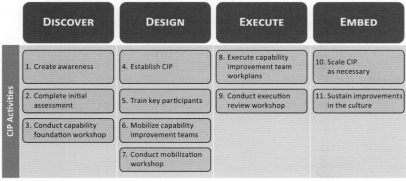

FIGURE 4: OVERVIEW OF CIP

CIP Phase 1: Discover

The first phase of a CIP is one of discovery that involves the leadership team in an organization agreeing on the business outcomes it expects to achieve with the CIP. This phase includes an 'initial assessment' that is chosen from the list of available formal assessments provided by IVI (See Appendix 1 for a list of available formal assessments) and that is appropriate to the organization's context and CIP aims.

Organizations that wish to start at a higher level and engage both business and IT professionals to create an initial CIP charter may use the rapid 'accelerator assessment' to help them review their current practices across a range of ten key business issues. And from there, they can define value propositions and identify the priority IT-CMF Critical Capabilities that might support them.

The 'accelerator assessment' is designed to be highly accessible to business professionals who are not necessarily technical experts, and for that reason it is organized around management issues rather than by the components of IT-CMF.

Figure 5 shows the key activities, tasks, and deliverables/outcomes for the Discover phase.

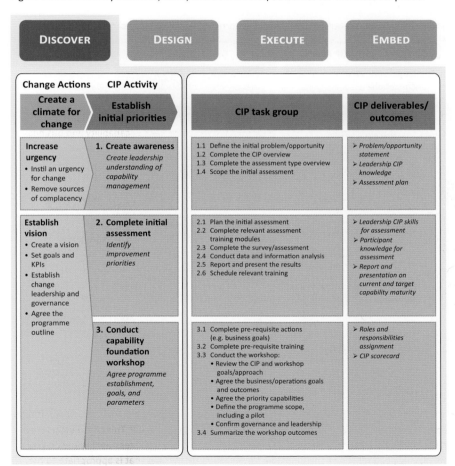

FIGURE 5: OVERVIEW OF THE CIP DISCOVER PHASE

CIP Phase 2: Design

The Design phase provides clear direction for the planning, training, and mobilization activities required to implement the outcomes formulated in the Discover phase. IVI provides a suite of tools and modules to train all participants, and this phase broadens the involvement from the CIP leadership team to include key improvement team leaders, subject matter experts, and other members of the capability improvement team.

Figure 6 shows the key activities, tasks, and deliverables/outcomes for the Design phase.

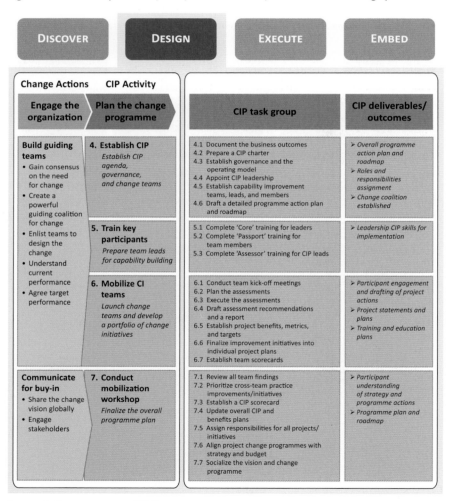

Change Actions	CIP Activity	CIP task group	CIP deliverables/outcomes
Engage the organization	**Plan the change programme**		
Build guiding teams • Gain consensus on the need for change • Create a powerful guiding coalition for change • Enlist teams to design the change • Understand current performance • Agree target performance	**4. Establish CIP** *Establish CIP agenda, governance, and change teams*	4.1 Document the business outcomes 4.2 Prepare a CIP charter 4.3 Establish governance and the operating model 4.4 Appoint CIP leadership 4.5 Establish capability improvement teams, leads, and members 4.6 Draft a detailed programme action plan and roadmap	➢ Overall programme action plan and roadmap ➢ Roles and responsibilities assignment ➢ Change coalition established
	5. Train key participants *Prepare team leads for capability building*	5.1 Complete 'Core' training for leaders 5.2 Complete 'Passport' training for team members 5.3 Complete 'Assessor' training for CIP leads	➢ Leadership CIP skills for implementation
	6. Mobilize CI teams *Launch change teams and develop a portfolio of change initiatives*	6.1 Conduct team kick-off meetings 6.2 Plan the assessments 6.3 Execute the assessments 6.4 Draft assessment recommendations and a report 6.5 Establish project benefits, metrics, and targets 6.6 Finalize improvement initiatives into individual project plans 6.7 Establish team scorecards	➢ Participant engagement and drafting of project actions ➢ Project statements and plans ➢ Training and education plans
Communicate for buy-in • Share the change vision globally • Engage stakeholders	**7. Conduct mobilization workshop** *Finalize the overall programme plan*	7.1 Review all team findings 7.2 Prioritize cross-team practice improvements/initiatives 7.3 Establish a CIP scorecard 7.4 Update overall CIP and benefits plans 7.5 Assign responsibilities for all projects/initiatives 7.6 Align project change programmes with strategy and budget 7.7 Socialize the vision and change programme	➢ Participant understanding of strategy and programme actions ➢ Programme plan and roadmap

FIGURE 6: OVERVIEW OF THE CIP DESIGN PHASE

CIP Phase 3: Execute

The purpose of the Execute phase is to support the organization in the implementation of its improvement plan. This is the phase in which the capability improvement team builds and improves the capabilities that matter to the organization – with guidance and support from IVI and subject matter experts. The Discover and Design phases are about establishing what are the right things to do; the Execute phase concentrates on doing the right things in the right way at the right time.

Figure 7 shows the key activities, tasks, and deliverables/outcomes for the Execute phase.

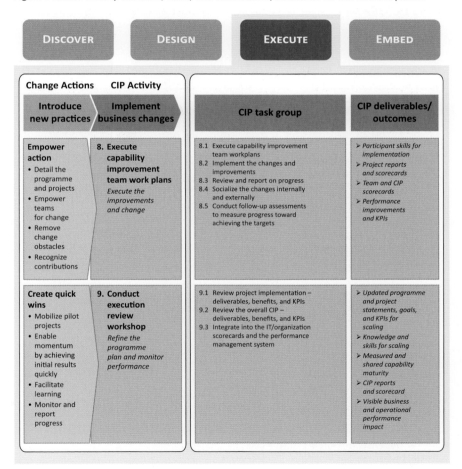

17

CIP Phase 4: Embed

The purpose of the Embed phase is to secure the gains and benefits from each improvement and improvement cycle, and scale the CIP as appropriate to the organization's programme plan. It's about institutionalizing the change and making it 'the way we do things'. This phase involves creating an ecosystem for continuous change and improvement that is dynamic and organic while still being properly governed and controlled. It means continuously making changes and improvements at individual, team, function, and organization level, and in an agile manner that assures their integrity and robustness.

Figure 8 shows the key activities, tasks, and deliverables/outcomes for the Embed phase.

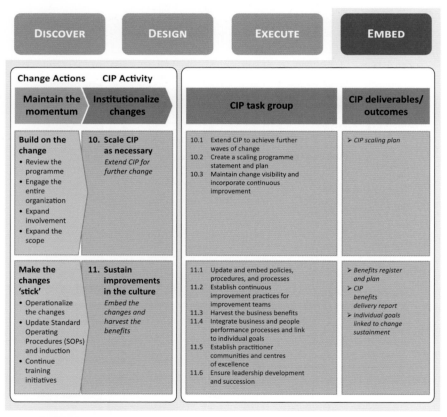

FIGURE 8: OVERVIEW OF THE CIP EMBED PHASE

About the Body of Knowledge Guide

IT-CMF offers organizations a wide range of practical guidance on how to manage all aspects of IT to best effect and to leverage IT investment so that it aligns with business goals. It is set on a firm foundation of peer-reviewed research and development experience that is encapsulated in *IT Capability Maturity Framework: The Body of Knowledge Guide* (2nd edition, 2016).

The Body of Knowledge Guide is a substantial and authoritative reference work that goes into considerably more detail than is possible in this *management guide*. It includes:

▶ Full references to the scholarly literature on IT management and practice.
▶ Detail on all five maturity levels for all of the Critical Capabilities.
▶ Representative *practices* for each maturity level for each Critical Capability, along with the *outcomes* that might result from them and the *metrics* against which they might be gauged.
▶ *Capability evaluation/assessment questions* that can help organizations determine their current and desired maturity levels in relation to each Critical Capability.
▶ Guidance on the interdependencies and relationships between Critical Capabilities that practitioners might take into account when designing a capability improvement programme.
▶ Information on the range of tools, templates, documents, software applications, and other *management artefacts* that can help organizations develop and mature their capabilities.

Notes

[1]   Helfat, C.E., and Peteraf, M.A., 2003. The dynamic resource-based view: capability lifecycles. *Strategic Management Journal*, 24(10), 997–1010.

[2]   Teece, D.J., 2007. Managers, markets, and dynamic capabilities. In C. Helfat, S. Finkelstein et al. (eds.), *Dynamic capabilities: understanding strategic change in organizations*. Oxford: Blackwell.

[3]   Mithas, S., Ramasubbu, N., and Sambamurthy, V., 2011. How information management capability influences firm performance. *MIS Quarterly*, 35(1), 237–56.

[4]   Nelson, R.R., and Winter, S.G., 1982. *An evolutionary theory of economic change*. Cambridge, MA: Belknap Press.

[5]   Porter, M.E., 1991. Towards a dynamic theory of strategy. *Strategic Management Journal*, 12, 95-117.

[6]   Dosi, G., Nelson, R.R., and Winter, S.G. (eds.), 2000. *The nature and dynamics of organizational capabilities*. Oxford: Oxford University Press.

[7]   Curley, M., 2004. *Managing information technology for business value*. Hillsboro, OR: Intel Press.

[8]   Eisenhardt, K.M., and Martin, J.A., 2000. Dynamic capabilities: what are they? *Strategic Management Journal*, 21(10/11), 1105–21.

[9]   Becker, J., Niehaves, B., Poppelbus, J., and Simons, A., 2010. Maturity models in IS research. In: *Proceedings of the 18th European conference on information systems*. Available at: <http://www.researchgate.net/publication/221408759_Maturity_Models_ in_IS_ Research>.

[10] Mettler, T., 2009. A design science research perspective on maturity models in Information Systems. Sankt Gallen: Institute of Information Management. University of Sankt Gallen, Switzerland.

[11] Humphrey, W.S., 1988. Characterizing the software process: a maturity framework. *IEEE Software*, 5(2), 73–9.

[12] Paulk, M.C., Curtis, B., Chrissis, M.B., and Weber, C., 1993. Capability maturity model for software (Version 1.). Software Engineering Institute. Available at <http://resources.sei. cmu.edu/library/asset-view.cfm?assetID=11955>.

[13] Curley, M., 2008. *The IT capability maturity framework: A theory for continuously improving the value delivered from IT capability*. Ph.D. National University of Ireland, Maynooth.

B. IT-CMF: Critical Capabilities

The numbered chapters in this section each relate to a particular Critical Capability (CC). In their layout and information design, these chapters are presented in a consistent manner, with the same content structure and headings. As you begin to use this book, you will become familiar with this structure and will find it easy to navigate through the different Critical Capabilities (CCs).

The structural components of each chapter are set out below.

Overview	Goal	The general purpose or end-state towards which the CC is directed.
	Objectives	Specifics regarding what the CC provides or enables. These provide the focus and the direction for the capability improvement effort.
Scope	Definition	A formal definition of the CC and its primary subject matter.
	Capability Building Blocks (CBBs)	The key components of the CC that enable its goals and objectives to be achieved efficiently and effectively. These are grouped into higher-order logical categories that are particular to each CC. For each CBB, there is a brief description of what it does.
Understanding Maturity and Planning Improvements	Recognizing Maturity Excellence	A brief description of what performance in the CC might look like when it is operating well, and how good performance can be recognized. The main characteristics of high performance are summarized here.
	Addressing Typical Challenges	Some typical IT management challenges are put in context for the reader and a recommended course of action is presented to address each of the listed challenges.

Managing IT like a Business

The **Managing IT like a Business** macro-capability provides a structure within which the IT function can be repositioned from a cost centre to a value centre. It comprises the following critical capabilities:

01	Accounting and Allocation (AA)
02	Business Planning (BP)
03	Business Process Management (BPM)
04	Capacity Forecasting and Planning (CFP)
05	Demand and Supply Management (DSM)
06	Enterprise Information Management (EIM)
07	Green IT (GIT)
08	Innovation Management (IM)
09	IT Leadership and Governance (ITG)
10	Organization Design and Planning (ODP)
11	Risk Management (RM)
12	Service Analytics and Intelligence (SAI)
13	Sourcing (SRC)
14	Strategic Planning (SP)

01. Accounting and Allocation

AA

01.1 AA: OVERVIEW

Goal
The Accounting and Allocation (AA) capability aims to allocate the consumption of IT services to business units and to calculate the associated costs for chargeback/showback purposes.

Objectives
▶ Promote better understanding of the cost drivers for IT services.
▶ Enable business units to fund directly the provision of new IT services that might not otherwise have occurred because of a limited IT budget.
▶ Motivate managers across the organization to make sound economic decisions – for example, by subsidizing newer systems and imposing additional charges for the use of legacy systems.
▶ Encourage users to avoid expensive IT activities when slightly less convenient but far cheaper alternatives are available.

01.2 AA: SCOPE

Definition
The Accounting and Allocation (AA) capability is the ability to define and manage the policies, processes, and tools used for calculating the costs of IT and distributing them across the organization.

Capability Building Blocks (CBBs)

The Accounting and Allocation (AA) capability comprises the following four Capability Building Blocks (CBBs), which fall into two categories.

Category	CBB	Definition
Category A: Model Development	CBB A1: Cost Coverage	Determine the scope of IT services (for example, essential, subscription, and discretionary services) whose costs are allocated to business units.
	CBB A2: Accounting Policy and Cost Recovery Model	Develop policies for calculating costs associated with the consumption of IT services, and develop a model for cost allocation and recovery.
Category B: Deployment	CBB B1: Decision-Making Transparency	Manage data on usage volumes and associated costs to provide visibility to inform decision-making across business units.
	CBB B2: Governance and Communication	Apply appropriate oversight and communication approaches to ensure that business unit stakeholders understand and have buy-in to cost allocation and recovery policies.

01.3 AA: UNDERSTANDING MATURITY AND PLANNING IMPROVEMENTS

Recognizing Maturity Excellence

When the Accounting and Allocation (AA) capability is well-developed or mature:

▶ Service usage and cost recovery policies are transparent and communicated to relevant stakeholders.

▶ Costs of IT services (including essential, subscription, and discretionary services) are accurately and fairly allocated to business units based on usage.

▶ There is automated and centralized management of cost information from federated Human Resources (HR), Enterprise Resource Planning (ERP), and other financial systems of record.

▶ IT accounting and allocation is used in strategic decision-making – for example, for investment planning, and for balancing between the variable and fixed costs associated with the provisioning of IT services.

Addressing Typical Challenges

Some typical challenges that can arise in attempting to develop maturity in the Accounting and Allocation (AA) capability are set out below.

Challenge	Lack of necessary tools and skills to implement accounting and allocation practices.
Context	Translating data from the Finance function into IT-relevant structures may require integrating disparate data sets and complex formulas.
Action	Implement a pilot cost accounting and allocation project, and build on it to develop a case for automating accounting and allocation processes. The best place to start is likely to be the area that causes the organization the most pain, or costs the most, or where the quickest return can be derived.
Challenge	Resistance from either the IT function or other business unit stakeholders.
Context	IT cost accounting and allocation may be seen as an unnecessary burden on the rest of the business. Initially, IT personnel may perceive the additional workload in a negative way and business units may resent having to pay for IT services.
Action	Encourage the senior management team to raise awareness of how cost accounting and allocation can empower business units to optimize the value they derive from their consumption of IT services.
Challenge	Lack of financial and consumption data to determine IT unit costs and usage.
Context	The investment required to consolidate financial records is not available.
Action	Work with the Finance function to determine a satisfactory level of detail in relation to IT service costs and business unit consumption, such that the effort of collecting the data is worthwhile.

02. Business Planning

02.1 BP: OVERVIEW

Goal

The IT function's Business Planning (BP) capability aims to link the IT strategy with IT operational planning. It represents the next level in planning detail following on from defining the IT strategy, ensuring that the necessary financial and other resources are allocated for implementation.

Objectives

▸ Break down the IT strategic plan into identifiable deliverables and required resources to achieve the medium- and long-term strategic objectives for the IT function.

▸ Build a robust process for allocating or reserving resources for IT programmes and operations in pursuit of strategic goals and objectives.

▸ Generate ownership and understanding among stakeholders of the critical success factors and the ways to monitor progress, so that the success of the IT business plan can be measured.

▸ Improve confidence that the IT function, through robust planning, can effectively deliver its goals and objectives within the specified planning period.

▸ Forecast the resources required to achieve the IT function's goals and objectives.

▸ Outline the financial and non-financial constraints within which the IT function operates.

▸ Focus and direct the IT effort by analysing actual against planned performance.

02.2 BP: SCOPE

Definition

The Business Planning (BP) capability is the ability to produce an approved document that provides implementable detail for the IT strategy, setting out the IT function's tactical objectives, the operational services to be provided, and the financial and other resources and constraints that apply in the coming planning period.

Capability Building Blocks (CBBs)

The Business Planning (BP) capability comprises the following ten Capability Building Blocks (CBBs), which fall into three categories.

Category	CBB	Definition
Category A: People	CBB A1: Roles and Responsibilities	Select employees with the experience, knowledge, and authority needed to represent the interests of stakeholders.
Category B: Process	CBB B1: Ongoing Operational Commitments	Determine the financial and other resources in the organization, and the extent to which they are already committed to ongoing contracts and obligations or are available to be deployed on new activities.
	CBB B2: Alignment Planning	Manage updates to the IT business plan to reflect changes in the IT strategy.
	CBB B3: Business Plan Development	Formulate, review, revise, canvass support for, finalize, and sign-off the IT business plan.
	CBB B4: Business Plan Communication	Communicate the IT business plan and its implications to stakeholders.
	CBB B5: Business Plan Review and Control	Monitor planned against actual performance, so that the plan can be adapted appropriately as business priorities change.
Category C: Content	CBB C1: Business Plan Objectives	Define IT objectives, including those relating to ongoing operational needs, new initiatives, and opportunities that the business wishes to pursue.
	CBB C2: Planned Resource Utilization	Forecast resources required to achieve the objectives set out in the IT business plan, including finance, equipment, facilities, energy, people, telecommunications, services, and so on.
	CBB C3: Success Criteria	Specify success criteria and associated metrics for determining the effectiveness of IT business planning.
	CBB C4: Planning Assumptions	Document the scope and provenance of the assumptions and estimates that underlie the IT business plan – for example, an internally generated sales forecast that is informed by market and customer feedback.

02.3 BP: UNDERSTANDING MATURITY AND PLANNING IMPROVEMENTS

Recognizing Maturity Excellence

When the Business Planning (BP) capability is well-developed or mature:

▶ The IT business plan expands on the IT strategic plan by identifying the required activities, their value propositions, and the resources needed to deliver them in a timely and efficient manner.

▶ Stakeholders can see the projected resource requirements and can see how their deployment will address objectives of the IT strategic plan.

▶ IT has a prioritized plan for activities and resources, balanced between current operational and future strategic needs.

▶ Potential expenditure efficiencies across business units can be identified, and resources can be allocated to the activities that are best aligned to the IT strategic plan.

▶ The relevancy of the IT business plan is proactively monitored and adjusted as required.

▶ The IT business plan is disseminated throughout the organization to inform resource allocation decisions, and to help IT employees understand how their work contributes to objectives specified in the IT strategy.

Addressing Typical Challenges

Some typical challenges that can arise in attempting to develop maturity in the Business Planning (BP) capability are set out below.

Challenge	The funding and resourcing provided are inadequate to support effective business planning.
Context	The organization does not see the value of IT business planning as the link between IT plans and the organization's strategic objectives is considered difficult to articulate.
Action	Demonstrate to management that business planning of IT is critical to realizing the organization's strategic objectives, and should be resourced accordingly.
Challenge	Limited availability of employees with sufficient experience and knowledge, and with sufficient authority to conduct IT business planning.
Context	There is a general shortage of employees suitable for IT business planning, often through a lack of focus on recruitment or poor in-house training and development.
Action	Initiate an awareness campaign on the importance of building skills in IT business planning using targeted recruitment and/or in-house training.

Challenge	Ensuring IT business planning serves the needs of other business units, as well as the IT function.
Context	At the requirements gathering stage, emphasis is exclusively placed on the needs of the IT function, with little consideration of the needs of other business units.
Action	When gathering requirements, involve stakeholders from both the IT function and other business units. This can help maintain a balanced and representative consideration of business unit perspectives.
Challenge	It may not be possible to meet expectations of deliverables with existing resources.
Context	Resource capacity is poorly understood throughout the organization, resulting in unrealistic expectations.
Action	Promote wider discussion among senior management on improving transparency into available resource capacity in order to set more realistic expectations for deliverables contained within the IT business plan.

BPM

03. Business Process Management

03.1 BPM: OVERVIEW

Goal
The Business Process Management (BPM) capability helps create an understanding of business activity flows so that they can be more readily understood and developed, and so that errors can be reduced and risks mitigated.

Objectives
▶ Enable the organization to be more capable of change.
▶ Drive a holistic approach to process improvement using a cross-functional and organization-wide perspective.
▶ Correct and improve complex, people-intensive processes before (potentially) automating them.
▶ Support a better understanding of processes and their objectives, which in turn leads to a more reliable and efficient execution of these processes.
▶ Provide graphical representations of processes to facilitate more effective discussion and collaboration between process performers, and between performers and managers.
▶ Make the strategic objectives of the organization more explicit and visible (for example, reliability and efficiency, product or service quality, business agility, and so on).

03.2 BPM: SCOPE

Definition
The Business Process Management (BPM) capability is the ability to identify, design, document, monitor, optimize, and assist in the execution of both existing and new organizational processes.

Capability Building Blocks (CBBs)

The Business Process Management (BPM) capability comprises the following eleven Capability Building Blocks (CBBs), which fall into two categories.

Category	CBB	Definition
Category A: Foundation	CBB A1: Strategy and Leadership	Establish strategies and plans to lead the development of process management activities.
	CBB A2: Support Organization and Personnel	Establish the structure, competences, roles, responsibilities, and resource levels to support process improvement activities.
	CBB A3: Standards and Methods	Establish a set of standards and methods for managing processes. These could include modelling standards, process notations, definitions of terminology to be used, improvement methods, process governance structures, and measures for determining value and the effectiveness of implementation.
	CBB A4: Technologies	Identify and implement technologies for documenting, organizing, and evaluating process improvements.
	CBB A5: Stakeholder Management	Generate understanding, motivation, and commitment to process management. This may include communication about process management approaches, success stories, lessons learned, potential value opportunities, and value realized.
Category B: Implementation	CBB B1: Scope of Implementation	Establish the breadth of processes to be managed. This is guided by the organizational context – for example, by the structure, strategies, priorities, and culture of the organization.
	CBB B2: Process Architecture	Document the organization's process architecture, using consistent terminology, precise definition of objectives, roles, flows, and relationships, and agreed protocols for process naming.
	CBB B3: Process Governance	Establish a governance structure for the processes being addressed. This might cover process ownership, decision rights, and measures to evaluate progress against process objectives.
	CBB B4: Process Improvement	Identify and use available methodologies for evaluating, redesigning, and improving how the organization works towards its desired outcomes.
	CBB B5: Process Automation	Use technologies to simulate, integrate, operationalize, and monitor business processes.
	CBB B6: The IT Contribution	Use the IT function's organization-wide perspective to drive the effectiveness of business process management.

03.3 BPM: UNDERSTANDING MATURITY AND PLANNING IMPROVEMENTS

Recognizing Maturity Excellence

When the Business Process Management (BPM) capability is well-developed or mature:

▸ Continual adaptation is seen as a natural condition, where organizational processes are modified in response to internal and external events.

▸ All organizational processes are owned, governed, and measured by clearly identified process owners; and the process owners are given the appropriate authority and are held accountable for process improvement and performance.

▸ Organizations can describe and quantify the impact of business process management practices on organizational performance.

Addressing Typical Challenges

Some typical challenges that can arise in attempting to develop maturity in the Business Process Management (BPM) capability are set out below.

Challenge	The prevalence of a silo culture with poor communication across business functions.
Context	Some organizations tend to be defined in functional silos or separate business units that can limit the return on investment from business process management efforts at an organizational level.
Action	Develop an organizational culture that encourages different business units to work in harmony, so that they eliminate potential competition between them, and overcome obstacles to cooperation.
Challenge	The failure of business process management to deliver tangible value, with the consequent risk that investment in it will be cut.
Context	Implementing business process management across the organization is a complex undertaking that requires considerable commitment of financial and other resources.
Action	Encourage senior management to commit to overcoming bureaucratic and cultural obstacles to business process management. Ensure the required expertise is in place for business process management implementation.
Challenge	Over-emphasis on process tools and methods, rather than on business value.
Context	Because of the complexity and scope of business process management there can be a tendency to focus on tools and methods, rather than on adding value to the organization. This can be particularly challenging when business process management is led by or biased towards a single business unit.
Action	Ensure business process management teams are representative of the wider organizational interests. Monitor process performance and prioritize a programme of process changes based on objective value contributions.

Challenge	Volatility or fragmentation of the working environment arising from significant organizational change – as can happen, for example, with start-ups, or with organizations undergoing significant change or crisis management.
Context	An organization that is living 'hand to mouth' is not usually in a position to give organizational priority to required medium- or longer-term changes.
Action	Start with simple and tactically focused management of the organization's processes. Concentrate on improvements that deliver quick wins and build upon early successes.

04. Capacity Forecasting and Planning

04.1 CFP: OVERVIEW

Goal

The Capacity Forecasting and Planning (CFP) capability aims to understand what resources will be required to support IT services based on current and projected organizational demands.

Objectives

- Increase knowledge about the IT resource capacity in order to predict bandwidth constraints.
- Scenario-model the impact of business strategies and forecasts on IT resources.
- Inform management of IT strategies – for example, about over- or under-capacity utilization, or about reassigning underutilized resources.

04.2 CFP: SCOPE

Definition

The Capacity Forecasting and Planning (CFP) capability is the ability to model and forecast demand for IT services, infrastructure, facilities, and people.

Capability Building Blocks (CBBs)

The Capacity Forecasting and Planning (CFP) capability comprises the following five Capability Building Blocks (CBBs), which fall into two categories.

Category	CBB	Definition
Category A: IT Capacity Modelling	CBB A1: Model Design	Define a model or set of models to forecast resource utilization across IT services, infrastructure, facilities, and people. Agree on assumptions and methodology, as well as error tolerances for each resource type.
	CBB A2: Model Maintenance	Monitor the modelling accuracy (for example, by comparing actual to forecast resource utilization) and manage efficiency (for example, automation and data availability) of IT capacity modelling. Refine and recalibrate the model's structure, parameters, and assumptions, as required to improve performance.
Category B: IT Capacity Planning	CBB B1: Input Management	Identify inputs required for IT capacity forecasting. Gather and validate input data for forecast scenarios.
	CBB B2: Production of Capacity Plans	Compile capacity plans to inform decision-making.
	CBB B3: Communication	Communicate the IT capacity plan to relevant stakeholders, and facilitate action to resolve shortages and/or over-capacity.

04.3 CFP: UNDERSTANDING MATURITY AND PLANNING IMPROVEMENTS

Recognizing Maturity Excellence

When the Capacity Forecasting and Planning (CFP) capability is well-developed or mature:

▶ Credible data is available on current capacity utilization.
▶ Transparent and objective assumptions can be agreed when determining the possible spectrum of future demand scenarios.
▶ A comprehensive set of integrated models is used to forecast future capacity requirements across all IT resources.
▶ Forecasting models can be continually calibrated for accuracy and efficiency.
▶ Key stakeholders have a clear understanding of what actions are required to address capacity issues.

Addressing Typical Challenges

Some typical challenges that can arise in attempting to develop maturity in the Capacity Forecasting and Planning (CFP) capability are set out below.

Challenge	Poor communication on IT capacity forecasting and planning between different parts of the IT function, and between the IT function and the rest of the business.
Context	There are fragmented short-term and localized capacity forecasting and planning approaches across the IT function and the broader organization. Facilitating centralized capacity planning is not prioritized by the organization.
Action	Promote awareness of the need for accurate forecasting and communication of the IT capacity plan, and encourage proactive collaborations and feedback on the plan from all levels of the organization.
Challenge	Poor understanding of the patterns of business demand for IT services, and this limits the effectiveness of IT capacity planning.
Context	The IT function does not take the time or does not have the expertise to understand the patterns of demand across the organization. Further, the rest of the business might not provide the required information in a timely manner.
Action	Focus on recruiting/developing people with the expertise to understand, interpret, and communicate historic, current, and likely future patterns of demand in the organization. Encourage business units to work with the IT function to share their knowledge, and to jointly collaborate on translating patterns of demand into realistic and flexible capacity plans that the organization can afford.
Challenge	Lack of an effective business planning cycle across the organization.
Context	The senior management team regard business planning as a low priority activity, and this has knock-on impacts on the availability of suitable inputs for IT capacity planning.
Action	Encourage senior management to take the lead to ensure an effective and integrated planning cycle is in place, one that proactively considers the need for IT capacity forecasting and planning.

DSM

05.1 DSM: OVERVIEW

Goal

The Demand and Supply Management (DSM) capability aims to balance the business demand for IT services and the supply of those services.

Objectives

▶ Strive for equilibrium between the demand for and the supply capacity of IT services.
▶ Arrive at an understanding of the total or aggregate demand for IT services, and meet this with a supply capacity that is fit for purpose and cost-effective.
▶ Forecast the impact of demand for IT services on the scalability of the supply pipeline.
▶ Maintain a balanced IT services portfolio so that current requirements for IT can be managed, and expected future requirements can be provided for.
▶ Understand how emerging technologies can replace or substitute current technologies, and open up new supply options.

05.2 DSM: SCOPE

Definition

The Demand and Supply Management (DSM) capability is the ability to manage the IT services portfolio in such a way that there is a balance between the demand for and the supply of IT services.

Capability Building Blocks (CBBs)

The Demand and Supply Management (DSM) capability comprises the following six Capability Building Blocks (CBBs), which fall into three categories.

Category	CBB	Definition
Category A: Demand Management	CBB A1: Demand Analysis and Management	Analyse business demand for and consumption of IT services to anticipate future demand and how it might be provided for.
	CBB A2: Technology Impact Assessment	Comprehend the impact that changes in emerging technologies could have on business demand for IT services.
Category B: Supply Management	CBB B1: Supply Analysis and Management	Gather and analyse information on the supply capacity of IT services to arrive at optimum supply solutions.
	CBB B2: Technology Application	Analyse existing and emerging technologies with a view to determining what are the most cost-effective supply solutions.
Category C: Equilibrium Management	CBB C1: Gap Management	Ensure IT services meet business needs by addressing projected gaps between the supply of IT services and likely business demand. This might include measures such as capacity expansion, changes in charging structures, product or service substitutions, training programmes for end users, and the association of incentives and penalties with particular usage patterns.
	CBB C2: Service Portfolio Management	Manage the IT services portfolio to include setting deployment schedules for new services, making changes to existing services, and removing redundant services.

05.3 DSM: UNDERSTANDING MATURITY AND PLANNING IMPROVEMENTS

Recognizing Maturity Excellence

When the Demand and Supply Management (DSM) capability is well-developed or mature:

- ▶ The IT function's ability to predict and meet demand for current and future IT services is enhanced.
- ▶ Shortfalls and surpluses of IT services are minimized – this occurs through the use of a balanced IT services portfolio that facilitates cost-effective development of new IT services and retirement of those that are no longer required.
- ▶ Decision-making in relation to demand and supply is informed by what-if analysis that assesses likely impact of different scenarios on demand or supply.
- ▶ Emerging technologies are rapidly and systematically applied to alleviate demand bubbles or supply shortfalls in IT service provision.

Addressing Typical Challenges

Some typical challenges that can arise in attempting to develop maturity in the Demand and Supply Management (DSM) capability are set out below.

Challenge	There are regular gaps between the anticipated demand and the actual supply of IT services.
Context	Identifying business demand levels doesn't involve the IT function.
Action	Indicate the adverse business and IT reputational damage that shortages or outages of services might have – for example, value at risk. Promote cross-functional collaboration, communication, and the use of shared operations diaries for the effective supply management of IT services to meet business demand.
Challenge	Other business units assume the supply of IT services to be instantaneous and infinite.
Context	IT service supply interdependencies are poorly understood by stakeholders, and this leads regularly to shortfalls or oversupply, and incurs costs that could be avoided.
Action	Promote collaboration between the IT function and the rest of the business on how best to ensure that the supply of IT services is cost-effective.

Challenge	Satisfying all of the business demand for IT services potentially inflates IT costs beyond what is appropriate to support business operations.
Context	Other business units may not understand the IT function's role in proposing effective and efficient IT service solutions.
Action	Promote cross-functional discussions on the strategies that other business units use to cope with volume fluctuations, and how the IT function could adapt some of these appropriately.

06. Enterprise Information Management

06.1 EIM: OVERVIEW

Goal

The Enterprise Information Management (EIM) capability ensures that quality data is available to support the business activities of the organization.

Objectives

▸ Improve the quality of information available at all levels of the organization to support improved decision-making and business insights.

▸ Improve the efficiency of business processes by making data and information available that is fit for purpose.

▸ Provide flexible, dynamic, and centralized data platforms that enable stakeholders to access, interpret, and manipulate data as appropriate to their roles.

▸ Enable the analysis of data and information to improve the identification and exploitation of new business opportunities by the provision of an appropriate linked data platform.

▸ Safely and effectively manage data and information throughout their life cycles.

06.2 EIM: SCOPE

Definition

The Enterprise Information Management (EIM) capability is the ability to establish effective systems for gathering, analysing, disseminating, exploiting, and disposing of data and information. The data can be held in any medium – all forms of digital storage, film, paper, or any other recording mechanism used by the organization.

Capability Building Blocks (CBBs)

The Enterprise Information Management (EIM) capability comprises the following sixteen Capability Building Blocks (CBBs), which fall into four categories.

Category	CBB	Definition
Category A: Strategy and Organization	CBB A1: Information Management Strategy	Define the long-term value and competitive positioning objectives for the management, sources, and uses of information.
	CBB A2: Information Governance	Develop and implement authorization and decision-making approaches that are executed through organizational structures and activities.
	CBB A3: Communities of Practice	Build, foster, and maintain the sharing of good information management practices among employees.
	CBB A4: Leadership	Promote the adoption of information management practices.
Category B: Standards, Policies, and Controls	CBB B1: Standards and Policies	Develop and communicate standards and policies for information management (including data definitions, taxonomies, models, usage patterns, archiving policies and schedules, information policies, roles and rights), and key process indicators (such as service levels for all data and information-based services, and cost of ownership).
	CBB B2: Controls	Establish a control framework for information management, which may include ways to monitor effectiveness and efficiency, manage change, and control access, as well as guidance on data and information use.

Category	CBB	Definition
Category C: Information Management	CBB C1: Information Valuation	Establish and update the value of data and information assets based on criteria such as economic, financial, reputational, and technical risk, age, frequency of use, and position within the information life cycle.
	CBB C2: Master Data Management	Define and maintain one or more master datasets, and synchronize them across relevant processes and systems. Define the data patterns and the quality standards to which data must conform in each stage of its life cycle.
	CBB C3: Metadata Management	Define and update metadata that indicates the information life cycle stage and access control criteria for both business and technical data.
	CBB C4: Information Quality	Establish policies that promote data and information quality.
	CBB C5: Information Life Cycle Management	Define and manage the life cycle for business, technical, and forensics data and information to ensure that it is accurate, available, and accessible, and that it is removed at the end of its useful life. Life cycle management extends to archive maintenance.
	CBB C6: Business Continuity Management	Provide information to business continuity planning on the data and information that is needed to support various business functions and activities.
	CBB C7: Information Security	Provide oversight, processes, and tools to enable the security, availability, integrity, and accessibility of information throughout its life cycles.
Category D: Enabling Business Analytics	CBB D1: Competences and Tools	Develop competences and tools for information management, business intelligence, and analytics to support decision-making.
	CBB D2: Data Provision	Provide data for reporting and analysis purposes.
	CBB D3: Reports and Analytics	Provide reports for representing and interpreting business information.

06.3 EIM: UNDERSTANDING MATURITY AND PLANNING IMPROVEMENTS

Recognizing Maturity Excellence

When the Enterprise Information Management (EIM) capability is well-developed or mature:

▶ Enterprise information is used strategically to support the goals and objectives of the organization, and its effective management is recognized as a top priority for business success.

▶ Business, technical, forensic, and operational information is maintained consistently and efficiently across the organization. Data is available to those who need it on a timely and cost-effective basis.

▶ There is an accessible data and information platform that facilitates analytics and business intelligence.

▶ The management and security of information is facilitated by appropriate metadata that classifies the data, specifies how it is to be managed through its life cycle, controls access to it, logs all access to it, and provides an audit trail.

Addressing Typical Challenges

Some typical challenges that can arise in attempting to develop maturity in the Enterprise Information Management (EIM) capability are set out below.

Challenge	Returns from investing in enterprise information management take time and are often not immediately realized.
Context	Organizational inertia may exist due to the perception that large efforts are needed to develop information management services.
Action	Work with key stakeholders to identify a small number of areas for quick wins with visible returns on investment. Continue with plans to incrementally build expertise, tools, and processes across the organization. Develop and win support for an enterprise information management strategy.
Challenge	Locally focused optimization efforts may yield quick savings but can impair a coherent approach to information management across the organization.
Context	An overarching strategy is lacking and funding is made available for individual projects, rather than at a portfolio level.
Action	Acknowledge localized work, but emphasize with senior management the need to develop an organization-wide approach. Define roles and assign owners and data stewards with organization-wide responsibilities.

Challenge	There is little support for the multi-year planning approach needed to resolve data and information issues.
Context	Designing and implementing master data and metadata sets can take a number of years.
Action	Seek senior management support for strategic data and information management goals by developing win-win scenarios across business units. Ensure employee rewards are not adversely affected by their work on longer-term strategic objectives.
Challenge	Difficulty in gaining consensus and support for data and information management activities that span the entire organization.
Context	Different parts of the organization own different data sets, and the ownership of data may change as it moves along its various life cycles. Access rights, data format needs, and other attributes may differ, depending on the intended use and purpose of the data.
Action	Build discussions and trust among key stakeholders as to the benefits of sharing data across the organization, and how it will lead to improved decision-making and insights. Identify and illustrate some quick wins to gain support.

07. Green Information Technology

07.1 GIT: OVERVIEW

Goal

The Green Information Technology (GIT) capability aims to manage IT operations in an environmentally sensitive manner, and to leverage IT to minimize the environmental impact of the wider business activities.

Objectives

▸ Enable the organization to meet its goals of minimizing its environmental impact by:
  ▸ Developing the IT capabilities to minimize the impact of computing activities on the environment – for example, sourcing/designing, operating, and disposing of the computing infrastructure efficiently and effectively with minimal or no impact on the environment.
  ▸ Enabling hi-tech/low-carbon business operations – for example, redesigning business operations using environmentally sensitive IT solutions.
▸ Enable the organization to comply with environmental regulations.
▸ Enhance its brand reputation by minimizing the organization's environmental impact.
▸ Demonstrate leadership in information technology practices that have environmental benefits (planet), social benefits (people), and financial benefits (profit).

07.2 GIT: SCOPE

Definition

The Green Information Technology (GIT) capability is the ability to minimize the environmental impact of IT, and to make the best use of technology to minimize environmental impact across the organization.

Capability Building Blocks (CBBs)

The Green Information Technology (GIT) capability comprises the following nine Capability Building Blocks (CBBs), which fall into four categories.

Category	CBB	Definition
Category A: Strategy and Planning	CBB A1: Objectives	Define the green information technology objectives for the IT function.
	CBB A2: Alignment	Align green information technology objectives between the IT function and the rest of the business.
Category B: Process Management	CBB B1: Operations and Life Cycle	Source/design, operate, and dispose of IT systems in an environmentally sensitive manner.
	CBB B2: Technology-Enhanced Business Processes	Identify IT solutions that enable environmentally sensitive business operations.
	CBB B3: Performance and Reporting	Demonstrate progress against objectives for green information technology concerning the IT function or technology-enabled solutions across business operations.
Category C: People and Culture	CBB C1: Language	Define, communicate, and use language and vocabulary for green information technology that are understood by all stakeholders.
	CBB C2: Adoption	Promote principles and behaviours that support green information technology.
Category D: Governance	CBB D1: Regulatory Compliance	Enable and demonstrate compliance with external standards and regulations concerning the environmental impact of computing and business operation activities.
	CBB D2: Corporate Policies	Establish corporate policies to support a green information technology strategy.

07.3 GIT: UNDERSTANDING MATURITY AND PLANNING IMPROVEMENTS

Recognizing Maturity Excellence

When the Green Information Technology (GIT) capability is well-developed or mature:

▶ Green information technology practices and solutions become increasingly integrated into the organization and are part of the overall business strategy.

▶ Achievement of environmental sustainability goals is both supported and influenced by IT.

▶ The organization consistently reviews its IT investment priorities to minimize environmental impact.

▶ Environmentally sustainable IT capabilities are adopted across the IT supply chain and business ecosystem, and suppliers are assessed against environmental sustainability goals.

Addressing Typical Challenges

Some typical challenges that can arise in attempting to develop maturity in the Green Information Technology (GIT) capability are set out below.

Challenge	Lack of organizational commitment and resources to support green information technology initiatives.
Context	Green information technology is seen as a low priority item by senior management – for example, because it might cost too much.
Action	Identify a sustainability champion who can demonstrate to senior management how green information technology can reduce costs, and enhance business reputation.
Challenge	Lack of confidence to deliver the green information technology strategy.
Context	Management and personnel do not have the required knowledge of green information technology, or struggle to see how it can be applied within the organization.
Action	Discuss how to increase expertise across the organization using training, HR policies, mentoring networks, a dedicated green information technology centre of excellence, and so on.
Challenge	Absent or limited involvement across the organization in planning and priority-setting for green information technology.
Context	Historically, sustainability approaches may have been considered too IT-centric and inadequately aligned with the objectives of the wider organization.
Action	Make senior management aware of the benefits that can accrue to the entire organization from planning and setting sustainability objectives – for example, through aggregating and sharing resources, eliminating duplication of effort, uncovering hidden opportunities for technology-enabled solutions, and so on.

Challenge	There is organization-wide apathy among employees towards the achievement of sustainability goals.
Context	While sustainability goals and initiatives may have been agreed at senior levels, individual employees don't feel engaged, motivated, or incentivized to help achieve them.
Action	Promote discussions on how individual employees can feel more ownership of the sustainability agenda through their engagement in shaping goals and initiatives, and by linking the achievement of sustainability goals to job performance appraisals. Provide employees with information on individual behaviours (for example, on energy and print consumption), organize regular seminars/training on environmentally sensitive behaviours, and so on.

08. Innovation Management

08.1 IM: OVERVIEW

Goal

The Innovation Management (IM) capability helps exploit IT in new and pioneering ways to satisfy business objectives.

Objectives

▸ Increase innovation throughput from the IT function by fostering a pioneering culture informed by approaches, methods, and tools for innovative thinking and problem solving.
▸ Incentivize collaboration with other business units to identify novel uses of IT to support business operations, products, and services.
▸ Improve accountability for innovation management by measuring business value and other meaningful metrics.
▸ Promote informed risk taking – for example, by:
  ▸ Harvesting key learnings from unsuccessful innovation initiatives using non-accusatory approaches.
  ▸ Supporting innovative performance of teams and individual employees.
  ▸ Providing more control over how employees approach solving business challenges.

08.2 IM: SCOPE

Definition

The Innovation Management (IM) capability is the ability to identify, fund, and measure technology-driven business innovation, which can be:

▸ Applied within the IT function.
▸ Applied to the organization's operations.
▸ Applied to the organization's products and services.

Capability Building Blocks (CBBs)

The Innovation Management (IM) capability comprises the following thirteen Capability Building Blocks (CBBs), which fall into three categories.

Category	CBB	Definition
Category A: Strategy and Management	CBB A1: Vision	Define, communicate, and realize the vision and goals for technology-driven innovation.
	CBB A2: Scope	Define the scope and nature of technology-driven innovation.
	CBB A3: Funding and Resource Allocation	Identify sources of funding for technology-driven innovation and allocate resources appropriately based on prioritization.
	CBB A4: Portfolio Management	Manage decision-making relating to technology-driven innovation projects through an innovation pipeline or portfolio.
Category B: People and Culture	CBB B1: Management Leadership	Provide visible leadership support for technology-driven innovation activities.
	CBB B2: Acceptance of Risk Taking	Promote a positive attitude towards informed risk-taking.
	CBB B3: Collaboration	Enable employee collaboration on technology-driven innovation – for example, task forces, cross-functional teams, collaboration networks, communities of practice, and so on.
	CBB B4: Innovation Skills Development	Develop employees' skills to enable and leverage technology-driven innovation.
	CBB B5: Roles and Responsibilities	Define roles and responsibilities within the organization to empower ownership of technology-driven innovation and promote engagement with innovation practices.
	CBB B6: Rewards and Recognition	Incentivize people to contribute to technology-driven innovation.
Category C: Methods and Measurement	CBB C1: Methods and Processes	Leverage methodologies and tools (such as idea management tools, innovation prototyping workshops, and project management methodologies) to facilitate an innovation management life cycle – for example, from idea generation and development to implementation and end-of-life.
	CBB C2: Measurement of Impact	Measure the impact from technology-driven innovation.
	CBB C3: Communication of Value	Communicate the value generated from technology-driven innovation.

08.3 IM: UNDERSTANDING MATURITY AND PLANNING IMPROVEMENTS

Recognizing Maturity Excellence

When the Innovation Management (IM) capability is well-developed or mature:

▶ The IT function demonstrates excellence in IT services and operations, and has won the right to own the agenda for technology-driven business innovation.

▶ There is a focus on continual improvement using a combination of business change and the power of IT to deliver technology-driven business innovation.

▶ The IT function understands the rest of the business from the perspective of the business leaders, and is proactive about promoting the capabilities of various technologies.

▶ There are enabling innovation management approaches that filter and nurture the ideas that have the best chance of breakthrough success – for example, through ideation, screening, rapid failure testing, and so on.

▶ The organization actively promotes a culture of innovation by the way in which it allocates resources such as funding, time, and people to improve innovation practices, by its strong leadership support of innovation, and by other means, including employee incentives. Informed risk-taking is regarded as an organizational strength; and nurturing technology-driven business innovation is considered part of everyone's job.

▶ Technology-driven business innovation enhances the reputation of the organization.

Addressing Typical Challenges

Some typical challenges that can arise in attempting to develop maturity in the Innovation Management (IM) capability are set out below.

Challenge	Scepticism that the IT function can credibly deliver a technology-driven innovation agenda.
Context	It can be difficult to own a technology-driven innovation agenda if the IT function is viewed merely as a utility provider, especially where the IT function struggles to provide basic IT services of an adequate quality.
Action	Build credibility with key stakeholders by ensuring IT operations are 'rock-solid' and reliably support stable IT services. Capitalize upon the IT function's growing reputation during strategic planning discussions to help grow a technology-driven innovation mandate.

Challenge	Lack of employee buy-in for technology-driven innovation.
Context	Technology-driven innovation is not always appropriately incentivized. Indeed, there may be significant deterrents that discourage employees from wanting to engage in innovation – for example, a negative career impact for ideas that don't work, or inappropriate performance metrics geared solely around day-to-day operations.
Action	Create an environment where innovation and innovative behaviours are encouraged (for example, by providing appropriate rewards) and enabled (for example, by ensuring there are no disincentives to engage in innovation).
Challenge	Potentially breakthrough technology-driven innovations fail to gain traction with key stakeholders.
Context	More radical ideas may not be understood by key stakeholders, who might not appreciate their potential value or who might consider them implausible, and this could result in missed business opportunities.
Action	Harness the commitment and energy of 'idea/innovation evangelists' to generate support for innovative ideas across the organization, and in doing so help key stakeholders to comprehend how such breakthrough technology-driven innovations could be realized. Additionally, stakeholder support for innovative initiatives can be increased by including them from the outset, getting their input at every phase so that the final outcome has been designed with the stakeholders' needs in mind.
Challenge	Striking the right balance between structured and unstructured approaches to managing technology-driven innovation.
Context	While guidelines, tools, and methods can help channel purposeful technology-driven innovation, imposing a structure that is too rigid may stifle ingenuity and creativity.
Action	Make a selection of approaches and frameworks available to manage technology-driven innovation, allowing flexibility in the type of approaches and frameworks that may be followed. Base such flexibility on the specific context of the various innovation efforts being undertaken.

Challenge	Reluctance to fund promising ideas that may be risky.
Context	There can be significant risks associated with innovation, with uncertain returns and unpredictable outcomes that may deter support for risky but potentially breakthrough ideas.
Action	Develop multiple funding sources and pipeline management strategies for technology-driven innovation projects, which will share investments and potential risks, and spread the intensity of innovation-related activities. For example, this could be achieved by staging investments so that they are tied to particular achievements, and thus lower risk incrementally.
Challenge	Unwillingness to increase funding (or stay the course) with promising or breakthrough innovations.
Context	While return on investment for technology-driven innovation may be promising, it might not materialize fast enough to satisfy the organization's financial criteria for current revenue flows.
Action	Create safe havens (for example, 'incubators', or even 'spin-offs') for relevant technology-driven innovation efforts that have potentially greater return on investment but over a longer time period. This will give the innovations a chance to get established and be protected from the organization's shorter-term financial analysis criteria.

ITG
09. IT Leadership and Governance

09.1 ITG: OVERVIEW

Goal
The IT Leadership and Governance (ITG) capability establishes a leadership style, and ensures that distributed IT decisions are supportive of the organization's strategic goals and objectives.

Objectives
▸ Establish the IT leadership competences required to drive organizational progress and win stakeholder support.
▸ Enhance the business orientation and engagement of IT leaders.
▸ Establish IT governance as a central component of effective corporate governance.
▸ Improve confidence in, and the agility and transparency of IT decision-making.
▸ Establish appropriate IT accountability mechanisms.
▸ Establish oversight structures to support compliance with ethical, legislative, and/or regulatory obligations.
▸ Provide broad oversight on the performance of IT in the organization.

09.2 ITG: SCOPE

Definition
The IT Leadership and Governance (ITG) capability is the ability to motivate employees towards a common strategic direction and value proposition, and to establish appropriate IT decision-making bodies and processes, including mechanisms for IT escalation, accountability, and oversight. While the leadership aspect establishes the IT function's direction, it cannot directly affect all IT decisions distributed across the various levels in the organization. The governance aspect addresses this by establishing appropriate IT decision rights, and mechanisms for accountability and oversight.

Capability Building Blocks (CBBs)

The IT Leadership and Governance (ITG) capability comprises the following eight Capability Building Blocks (CBBs), which fall into two categories.

Category	CBB	Definition
Category A: Leadership	CBB A1: Value Orientation	Advocate for delivery of the expected business value from IT.
	CBB A2: Business Interaction	Build a high-quality and effective partnership between the IT function and other business units. Build an understanding of business requirements and how they can be met or enabled by IT.
	CBB A3: Communication	Establish mechanisms for dialogue with stakeholders such as IT colleagues, other business units, and third parties.
	CBB A4: IT Vision	Promote the role of the IT function and its strategic direction.
	CBB A5: Style, Culture, and Collaboration	Create a style of IT leadership that is effective in driving progress, winning support from stakeholders, and fostering a culture of credibility, accountability, and teamwork.
Category B: Governance	CBB B1: Decision Bodies and Escalation	Establish IT governance bodies, defining their composition, scope, and decision rights, stating their role in complying with regulatory obligations, and setting out protocols for escalation between them and their organizational units.
	CBB B2: Decision-Making Processes	Implement decision-making processes based on, for example, principles of transparency and accessibility. Document decisions and translate them into action plans.
	CBB B3: Reporting and Oversight	Monitor the status of essential IT capabilities and desired outcomes, including key performance indicators (KPIs) and accountabilities.

09.3 ITG: UNDERSTANDING MATURITY AND PLANNING IMPROVEMENTS

Recognizing Maturity Excellence

When the IT Leadership and Governance (ITG) capability is well-developed or mature:

▸ IT leadership steers the IT function in a direction that supports the organization's strategic goals and objectives.

▸ IT leadership drives a culture within the IT function that distributes decision-making and accountability to high-performing individuals and teams.

▸ The IT function works effectively with other business units. IT governance decisions are jointly taken by IT and other business unit leaders.

▸ IT governance bodies employ transparent decision-making structures and approaches to support organizational objectives.

▸ Accountabilities for value delivery are defined and assigned for all projects across the organization, are systematically tracked with respect to individual and group performance, and are continually optimized.

Addressing Typical Challenges

Some typical challenges that can arise in attempting to develop maturity in the IT Leadership and Governance (ITG) capability are set out below.

Challenge	Undervaluing the importance of inspiring employees with the IT vision.
Context	Promotion of the IT function's direction and vision is not considered important by other organizational stakeholders.
Action	Stimulate senior management awareness and discussion on the importance of providing clarity, motivation, and buy-in in relation to the vision for the IT function and its connection to wider business objectives.
Challenge	Evidence of inadequate IT leadership to support the organization's goals and objectives.
Context	IT leadership lacks credibility within the IT function and with the wider organization due to an inability to deliver projects, foster teamwork, and define accountability.
Action	Stimulate senior management discussion on how the IT leadership style can support organizational progress, fostering a culture of commitment and accountability.

Challenge	Poor understanding of the IT function's value proposition and the business value that it can deliver.
Context	The IT function's image is one of a technology implementer, rather than a contributor to the broader organization's strategic direction and business value realization.
Action	Promote widespread awareness and visibility across the senior management team of how the IT function has contributed and can contribute to business success.
Challenge	Lack of alignment between the IT function's activities and the business objectives.
Context	The IT function's role in supporting business objectives is not clearly defined. The IT function's activities are often considered in isolation from the objectives of the business.
Action	Promote a partnership-type relationship between the IT function and other business units, in which they both recognize the importance of developing a shared understanding of business requirements and how they can be enabled by IT.
Challenge	Underestimating the importance of IT governance structures.
Context	IT governance is isolated from corporate governance structures. Transparent IT reporting lines, decision-making processes, roles, responsibilities, and accountabilities are not evident.
Action	Initiate an awareness campaign on the importance of IT governance in consistently supporting day-to-day activities to deliver successful outcomes.
Challenge	A lack of senior business management support and buy-in to IT governance.
Context	Current IT governance structures are too complex or have little or no transparency. Control aspects are over-emphasized, and too little focus is placed on deriving business value.
Action	Foster a senior management mind-set that recognizes effective and agile IT governance as central to the organization's competitiveness and business success.
Challenge	Lack of an escalation process to support effective IT decision-making.
Context	IT decisions are not escalated to an appropriate individual or level in the organization. Hence, the decisions made may not be the most effective for enabling the organization to achieve its goals.
Action	Raise awareness of the importance of establishing escalation structures and supporting mechanisms to enable IT decisions to be made in a consistent and timely manner.

10. Organization Design and Planning

10.1 ODP: OVERVIEW

Goal

The Organization Design and Planning (ODP) capability aims to organize the IT function by establishing lines of authority, defining roles and functions, and specifying their interrelationships, so that IT employees can collectively deliver the objectives of the IT function.

Objectives

▶ Promote effective decision-making and follow-on action by removing organizational bureaucracy and structural inefficiencies.
▶ Ensure that the organization design of the IT function is appropriate to the wider organization it serves.
▶ Promote IT employees' acceptance of organizational change.
▶ Clarify reporting lines, roles, responsibilities, and accountabilities.
▶ Organize the IT function so that it can develop and leverage core IT capabilities.

10.2 ODP: SCOPE

Definition

The Organization Design and Planning (ODP) capability is the ability to manage the IT function's internal structure and its interfaces with other business units, suppliers, and business partners.

Capability Building Blocks (CBBs)

The Organization Design and Planning (ODP) capability comprises the following six Capability Building Blocks (CBBs), which fall into two categories.

Category	CBB	Definition
Category A: Organization Design	CBB A1: Internal Structure	Define the internal structure of the IT function so that it supports the organization's strategic direction and culture. The definition includes, for example, reporting lines, roles, responsibilities, accountabilities, and span of control (that is, the number of employees reporting to each manager).
	CBB A2: Business Interfaces	Manage the interfaces between the IT function and other business units.
	CBB A3: Supplier Interfaces	Manage the interfaces between the IT function and its suppliers.
Category B: Organization Planning	CBB B1: Planning Process	Manage the organizational planning process for the IT function and the outcomes of that process, for example by involving stakeholders, and securing commitment to change.
	CBB B2: Documentation and Communication	Document the IT function's organization design (including, for example, an organization chart showing links between units and interfaces), and communicate it to relevant stakeholders.
	CBB B3: Monitoring	Monitor the effectiveness of the IT function's organization design.

10.3 ODP: UNDERSTANDING MATURITY AND PLANNING IMPROVEMENTS

Recognizing Maturity Excellence

When the Organization Design and Planning (ODP) capability is well-developed or mature:

▸ The IT function's organization structure is arranged in such a way that it supports the strategic direction of the wider organization.

▸ The IT function's organization structure is highly responsive to business and operating environment changes, and to strategic leadership goals.

▸ The IT function is able to adopt different organization structures to meet business needs, and the structures are regularly optimized.

▸ All interfaces between the IT function and other business units, suppliers, and business partners are formally designed, monitored, and adapted as required.

▸ Decision rights, accountabilities, and responsibilities are documented.

▸ KPIs are agreed for measuring the effectiveness of the organization design of the IT function, and regular monitoring occurs.

Addressing Typical Challenges

Some typical challenges that can arise in attempting to develop maturity in the Organization Design and Planning (ODP) capability are set out below.

Challenge	Poor awareness of the factors that influence the design of an effective organization structure.
Context	The importance of the business context and operating environment is not recognized when designing new organization structures – for example, political influences can dictate new organization structures.
Action	Stimulate discussion among senior management on how organization design needs to take the business context into account if it is to be effective.
Challenge	Inability to formalize the design of interfaces with other business units, suppliers, and business partners.
Context	A lack of shared responsibilities and poorly defined task descriptions make it more difficult to design and operationalize interfaces.
Action	Promote greater collaboration between relevant stakeholders in the IT function, other business units, suppliers, and business partners on the effective design of key interfaces.

Challenge	Resistance to organizational change and a desire to maintain the legacy organization structure of the IT function.
Context	The organization design does not engage sufficiently with stakeholders, resulting in lack of ownership and poor buy-in among employees.
Action	Initiate an awareness campaign on the rationale for organizational change. Seek appropriate stakeholder involvement in designing the new organization structure for the IT function. Communicate roles, responsibilities, and accountabilities to affected employees at the earliest opportunity.

RM
11. Risk Management

11.1 RM: OVERVIEW

Goal
The Risk Management (RM) capability aims to protect the organization from risk exposures associated with information technology (IT).

Objectives
▸ Identify and assess the IT-related risks that present vulnerabilities to the business, determine appropriate risk handling strategies, and monitor their effectiveness.
▸ Manage the exposure to IT-related risks such as those related to IT security, IT sabotage, data protection, information privacy, product and project life cycles, and IT investment; and protect the business from the impact of risk incidents.
▸ Increase compliance with external regulations and ethics policies relating to the deployment and use of technology.
▸ Increase transparency around how IT-related risks could affect business objectives and decisions.
▸ Contribute to improving the organization's reputation as a trusted supply chain business partner.

11.2 RM: SCOPE

Definition
The Risk Management (RM) capability is the ability to assess, prioritize, handle, and monitor the exposure to and the potential impact of IT-related risks that can directly impact the business in a financial or reputational manner. Risks include those associated with (among others) IT security, data protection and information privacy, operations, continuity of business and recovery from declared disasters, IT investment and project delivery, and IT service contracts and suppliers.

Capability Building Blocks (CBBs)

The Risk Management (RM) capability comprises the following ten Capability Building Blocks (CBBs), which fall into three categories.

Category	CBB	Definition
Category A: Governance	CBB A1: Policies for Risk Management	Define, implement, review, and make accessible risk management policies. Incorporate compliance requirements into risk management approaches.
	CBB A2: Integration	Integrate IT risk management with IT leadership and governance structures, and with overall ERM policies and approaches.
	CBB A3: Risk Management Programme and Performance Management	Identify risk management leadership responsibilities and accountability. Define risk management roles, responsibilities, and accountabilities in support of the programme's principles and guidance. Measure and report on the effectiveness and efficiency of risk management activities.
	CBB A4: Communication and Training	Disseminate risk management approaches, policies, and results. Train stakeholders in risk management practices. Develop a risk management culture and risk management knowledge and skills.
Category B: Profiling and Coverage	CBB B1: Definition of Risk Profiles	Define the risk profiles by their potential impact on business continuity and performance. Apply risk profiles in risk management activities.
	CBB B2: Risk Coverage	Establish the breadth of IT risk categories and asset classes that are addressed by risk management activities.
Category C: Process	CBB C1: Assessment	Identify subject matter experts for risk assessments. Run risk assessments to identify, document, and quantify or score risks and their components. Assessments include the evaluation of exposure to risks and measurement of their potential impact.
	CBB C2: Prioritization	Prioritize inherent and residual risks and risk handling strategies, based on the organization's risk tolerance – that is, what risk levels are acceptable.
	CBB C3: Handling	Assign ownership to identified risks, and responsibility and accountability for developing risk handling strategies. Initiate implementation of risk handling strategies, where risks can be transferred, absorbed, or mitigated. Interact with incident management functions.
	CBB C4: Monitoring	Establish a risk register. Track and report risks and risk incidents, and validate the effectiveness of risk controls.

11.3 RM: UNDERSTANDING MATURITY AND PLANNING IMPROVEMENTS

Recognizing Maturity Excellence

When the Risk Management (RM) capability is well-developed or mature:

▶ The risk management programme and framework are continually refined and updated in cooperation with other business units and relevant business ecosystem partners.

▶ Key IT risks are known, their likelihood and potential business impact are quantified, and appropriate risk handling strategies are in place (that is, the decision has been taken to accept, avoid, mitigate, or transfer them).

▶ Risks are effectively identified, tracked, and monitored, and lessons learned are incorporated into future risk management activities.

▶ Risk management is built into all relevant processes within the organization. The risk management of IT is integrated into wider ERM practices.

▶ Current and emerging risks associated with IT are continually identified and effectively managed.

▶ Risk management budget and resources are allocated effectively and efficiently.

▶ The efficacy of the Risk Management (RM) capability is confirmed at regular intervals.

Addressing Typical Challenges

Some typical challenges that can arise in attempting to develop maturity in the Risk Management (RM) capability are set out below.

Challenge	Provision of adequate funding and resourcing for an effective Risk Management (RM) capability.
Context	Identified risks can be difficult to quantify, and the value of risk management activities is measurable only in relation to the impacts of incidents that might never materialize. This may undermine the recognition of the need or desire for a Risk Management (RM) capability.
Action	Effective risk management of IT should be viewed as a necessary management activity, and should be funded as a component of the organization's overall approach to ERM.

Challenge	A lack of senior management ownership of risk management.
Context	Risk management is considered a low priority by the senior management team, seen as 'insurance' or an activity that does not add value to the core business.
Action	Stimulate a mind-set whereby effective risk management of IT is viewed as a value-add (or value-protection) activity and is funded as a component of the organization's overall approach to ERM.
Challenge	A general lack of awareness towards how risks associated with IT should be managed.
Context	There is limited understanding of risk management principles, tools, and techniques, or the skills required to manage risk effectively. Risk assessment, prioritization, handling, and monitoring approaches may or may not be in use.
Action	Initiate an awareness raising campaign on the importance of risk management in day-to-day activities to protect the organization.
Challenge	Difficulties in understanding and keeping up to date with current and emerging risks.
Context	The risks associated with IT are continually changing and evolving, sometimes remaining unknown until a breach is reported.
Action	Stimulate organizational commitment to proactively conducting outreach and horizon scanning initiatives with a view to understanding current and emerging risks.
Challenge	Risk management of IT is isolated from general business risk management.
Context	A reactionary, survivability stance prevails with respect to the risk management of IT.
Action	Promote greater collaboration between general business risk managers and those responsible for the management of risk associated with IT.

SAI

12. Service Analytics and Intelligence

12.1 SAI: OVERVIEW

Goal

The Service Analytics and Intelligence (SAI) capability aims to clarify the link between the performance of business processes and the performance of the underlying IT infrastructure and services – that is, to provide an end-to-end view of IT services.

Objectives

▶ Provide a quantified view of the end-to-end performance of IT services – that is, define and measure the relationship between IT infrastructure and services, and the business processes and services enabled by IT.

▶ Map performance data from discrete IT systems (including networks, finance, voice, data, storage, processing speeds, data centres, and applications) to performance data from business processes and services, to highlight business value-at-risk, gain insights into ways of optimizing IT infrastructure and service configurations, and prioritize future investments.

▶ Establish proactive approaches to resolving IT infrastructure and service quality problems by maintaining profiles of normal infrastructure operational characteristics, and automatically detecting deviations from norms.

▶ Support improved decision-making on the performance of IT services at all levels of the organization – that is:

  ▶ Inform operational decision-making relating to service delivery by providing insight into matters such as performance, capacity, availability, cost, and use.

  ▶ Inform strategic decision-making by providing insight into matters such as profiling of user populations, understanding the business impact of change, and contingency planning.

12.2 SAI: SCOPE

Definition
The Service Analytics and Intelligence (SAI) capability is the ability to define and quantify the relationships between IT infrastructure, IT services, and IT-enabled business processes.

Capability Building Blocks (CBBs)
The Service Analytics and Intelligence (SAI) capability comprises the following eight Capability Building Blocks (CBBs), which fall into three categories.

Category	CBB	Definition
Category A: Profiling	CBB A1: Empirical Model	Define and quantify the relationships between IT infrastructure (for example, CPU load or latency) and IT services, business processes, and ultimately, the organization. Populate models with data to act as a basis for all analysis (including historical and projected).
	CBB A2: Performance Monitoring	Measure, record, and track various service performance indicators for IT infrastructure, end-to-end IT services, business processes, and the organization (based on empirical models).
	CBB A3: Results Analysis	Identify the key issues relating to IT infrastructure and how they impact or are impacted by IT services, business processes, and the organization, based on empirical model outputs.
Category B: Planning	CBB B1: Capacity Trend Analysis	Size the infrastructure based on current and expected business demand – for example, by examining current performance trends or deducing expected capacity needs from the business strategy.
	CBB B2: Risk Assessment	Assess the probability and impact of IT-related risks on organizational activities – for example, quantification of IT-enabled business value-at-risk.
	CBB B3: Investment Scenario Planning	Understand existing capacity and identify the need for additional/new IT infrastructure to support growth of business processes.
Category C: Business Interaction	CBB C1: Communication Management	Establish lines of communication between the IT function and other business units regarding the management of IT infrastructure and services.
	CBB C2: Partnership Management	Establish ways of managing and maintaining interactions with business units and stakeholders – these could include informal approaches, such as phone calls, emails, and courtesy visits, and formal written, signed agreements reviewed periodically.

12.3 SAI: UNDERSTANDING MATURITY AND PLANNING IMPROVEMENTS

Recognizing Maturity Excellence

When the Service Analytics and Intelligence (SAI) capability is well-developed or mature:

▸ There is a clear understanding of the relationship between the performance of business processes and the performance of the underlying IT infrastructure and services.

▸ Emerging trends can be identified and responded to before they become problems across the portfolio of IT services.

▸ Service analytics and intelligence is leveraged as part of strategic planning organization-wide (including in risk management, and investment planning).

Addressing Typical Challenges

Some typical challenges that can arise in attempting to develop maturity in the Service Analytics and Intelligence (SAI) capability are set out below.

Challenge	Analytical initiatives fail to gain traction across the wider organization.
Context	Senior management support is lacking in other business units owing to a lack of understanding regarding what can be achieved. Furthermore, analytical skills and expertise are inadequate to deliver such initiatives.
Action	In discussions with management, highlight business framed scenarios where analytics can help overcome existing business challenges or anticipate emerging trends before they pose significant business challenges. Prioritize recruitment and employee development programmes targeting appropriate analytical skills.
Challenge	Difficulty in accessing sufficient data for analysis and modelling.
Context	Infrastructure performance data can be difficult to compile, as it can reside deep inside technology stacks, in varying formats across heterogeneous systems and organizational boundaries.
Action	Initiate dialogue on the business value of extracting the required data either by in-house development or by using commercial off-the-shelf applications.
Challenge	It is difficult to achieve a consistent organization-wide approach to analytics.
Context	Analytics is largely viewed as an individual or business unit activity, with responsibility allocated to disparate groups or employees across the organization. This results in localized or fragmented approaches, leading to short-term local gains but hindering potentially larger organization-wide gains.
Action	Generate dialogue on the benefits of managing analytics at an organizational level, ensuring no one business process is optimized at the expense of another – unless it is strategically important to do so. Ensure proper care is taken to manage data and its analysis across the organization.

SRC
13. Sourcing

13.1 SRC: OVERVIEW

Goal
The Sourcing (SRC) capability aims to streamline the strategic planning and development of the IT supply base to optimize the contribution of the supply base to the organization's strategic objectives.

Objectives
▶ Establish a common approach to selecting IT suppliers for their operational contribution and potential strategic impact, instead of awarding contracts only or mainly on the basis of lowest bid price.

▶ Assess the value and relevance of current and potential sourcing opportunities and relationships according to long-term goals and overall business and supply management objectives.

▶ Achieve both cost reduction and improvement in IT supplier performance.

▶ Ensure continuity of supply if a supplier's operations are unexpectedly disrupted or when switching suppliers.

▶ Leverage good practice and innovations from the supply base to support business innovation.

▶ Increase organizational effectiveness by simplifying, automating, and integrating sourcing processes across the organization.

13.2 SRC: SCOPE

Definition
The Sourcing (SRC) capability is the ability to evaluate, select, and integrate IT service providers according to a defined strategy and sourcing model, which could include service providers both inside and outside the organization.

Capability Building Blocks (CBBs)

The Sourcing (SRC) capability comprises the following ten Capability Building Blocks (CBBs), which fall into three categories.

Category	CBB	Definition
Category A: Sourcing Strategy	CBB A1: Strategy Alignment	Align IT sourcing options and activities with the IT strategy for organizational impact.
	CBB A2: Objectives and Scoping	Specify the sourcing objectives (for example, quality, cost, flexibility, risk, innovation, agility), the scope of IT services, and the criteria used to evaluate and select service providers.
	CBB A3: Sourcing Model Selection	Choose appropriate sourcing model(s) to support delivery of IT services (for example, internal or third-party providers, single or multiple providers).
	CBB A4: Business Case Creation	Create and review business cases for evaluating sourcing options for IT services.
	CBB A5: Organizational Readiness	Assess and review the organization's readiness for sourcing initiatives. Such an assessment might take into account, for example, the extent of process standardization, the adaptability of the organizational structure and culture, the methods and media used for communication, and the policies and practices relating to resourcing and skills transfer and retention.
	CBB A6: Re-evaluation	Assess legacy sourcing decisions and consider alternative sourcing options. Consider, for example, changes that have taken place in the business context, new opportunities and risks that have arisen, and costs associated with vendor lock-in or switching.
Category B: Contracting	CBB B1: Provider Selection	Ensure that the approach used for selecting IT service providers adheres to and influences the organization's procurement procedures.
	CBB B2: Contract Preparation and Closing	Develop IT's own contract negotiation position in advance (for example, by identifying negotiable and non-negotiable items, and considering incentives). Understand the IT service provider's success criteria to create win-win situations.

Category C: Sourcing Execution	CBB C1: Transition	Support the introduction of new IT services or the migration of legacy IT services between the IT service provider and the organization, considering, for example, staffing the project team, identifying and informing affected employees, employee placement, preparing technical interfaces, migrating data, security protocols, defining access rights, and validating availability.
	CBB C2: Provider Integration and Governance	Integrate IT service providers into organizational activities with appropriate governance and performance oversight structures.

13.3 SRC: UNDERSTANDING MATURITY AND PLANNING IMPROVEMENTS

Recognizing Maturity Excellence

When the Sourcing (SRC) capability is well-developed or mature:

▸ There is an IT sourcing strategy that is aligned with the organization's overall business sourcing strategy.

▸ Rather than always demanding the lowest possible price, the organization can innovate with suppliers to transform the underlying cost structure of IT services.

▸ The intellectual capital of the supplier base is leveraged to develop new solutions, helping to influence – not just support – the organization's business strategy.

▸ The IT function protects the business from risk by working with stakeholders to determine the best mitigation strategy when a risk exposure is identified.

▸ Sourcing options for a range of IT services are regularly evaluated.

▸ The process for selecting IT service providers is aligned with an organization-wide sourcing approach to realize synergies.

▸ Commercial terms with IT service providers incentivize actions that are mutually beneficial.

▸ The sourcing governance model promotes sustainable, cooperative, and amicable relationships with IT service providers.

Addressing Typical Challenges

Some typical challenges that can arise in attempting to develop maturity in the Sourcing (SRC) capability are set out below.

Challenge	The IT sourcing model cannot adequately facilitate the central sourcing of all IT services across the entire organization, leading to rising 'shadow' IT expenditure.
Context	The IT function focuses primarily on stable sourcing arrangements that deliver robust and efficient back-office systems, while the other business units focus primarily on flexible sourcing arrangements that facilitate agile prototyping of front-office digital technologies, such as data analytics, mobility, and social media.
Action	Stimulate cross-organization discussions on how best to adopt IT sourcing models that can cater for both traditional and emerging business requirements for IT services – for example, by embracing a greater diversity of vendors, ranging from traditional hardware suppliers and system integrators to more innovative cloud service providers and entrepreneurial vendors.
Challenge	There is a fear that, once the organization selects a vendor, it will be *locked in* and unable to take advantage of innovations coming from other sources without incurring high switching costs, because of proprietary or non-standard vendor technologies.
Context	In many instances, there are, as yet, no widely accepted standards that promote interoperability between vendor offerings. This often means choosing between vendors of proprietary technologies (with the risk that the chosen vendor will take advantage of the arrangement) or choosing a consortium that is building open source technologies, in the hope that these will become dominant in the market.
Action	Investigate how the prospective vendor's technology can interface with external technologies, and the implications of migrating off it at a later point if it proves to be unsatisfactory. Factors to consider include data export formats, application programming interfaces (APIs), level of customization options, and use of open standards and protocols.
Challenge	Inability to conduct appropriate due diligence of commercial arrangements with potential IT service providers.
Context	The role of procuring IT services is not adequately resourced to deal with complex legal issues, sustainability concerns, or regulatory or ethical considerations.
Action	Canvass senior business leaders for their support for an adequately resourced IT procurement approach by highlighting the benefits in terms of managing and anticipating risk, and increasing transparency.

Challenge	Despite having been selected following rigorous evaluation, an IT service provider may fail to deliver against the stated business case, resulting in premature contract termination or renegotiation.
Context	With the shift to sourcing a significant proportion of IT services externally, the IT function lacks the skills required to manage external vendors effectively.
Action	Initiate discussions with senior management on such things as the methods, structures, incentives, and competences that are needed to proactively manage IT service providers so that they deliver innovation and business value.

SP

14. Strategic Planning

14.1 SP: OVERVIEW

Goal
The Strategic Planning (SP) capability aims to specify ways in which technology can enable and influence the business strategy.

Objectives

▸ Outline key strategic issues and options for how technology can support and influence the business strategy.

▸ Clarify the purpose and goals of IT activities, thus enabling more consistent decision-making.

▸ Align the IT function and other business units on the strategic value of technology to amplify the creation of business value.

▸ Translate strategy and decisions into a set of programmes calculated to deliver desired objectives.

▸ Clearly communicate strategic goals and targets to all stakeholders.

▸ Promote more effective and efficient technology deployments.

14.2 SP: SCOPE

Definition
The Strategic Planning (SP) capability is the ability to formulate a long-term vision and translate it into an actionable strategic plan for the IT function.

Capability Building Blocks (CBBs)

The Strategic Planning (SP) capability comprises the following eight Capability Building Blocks (CBBs), which fall into two categories.

Category	CBB	Definition
Category A: Embedding IT Strategic Planning in the Organization	CBB A1: Resourcing	Allocate and coordinate roles, responsibilities, accountabilities, and resources for the IT strategic planning function.
	CBB A2: Related Planning Processes	Align and integrate IT strategic planning with relevant IT and business planning processes, such as budget and operational planning, resource allocation, business planning, and performance measurements.
	CBB A3: Stakeholder Management and Communication	Communicate all aspects of IT strategic planning with stakeholders, including key individuals in the IT function, and business unit heads. Manage stakeholder expectations, engagement, and sponsorship.
Category B: Strategic Process	CBB B1: Alignment with Business	Mutually align and integrate IT and business strategic plans. Determine the IT strategy's contribution to business objectives. Influence the formation of the business strategy regarding the use of technology-enabled solutions to overcome business challenges.
	CBB B2: IT Vision and Principles	Formulate the long-term scope and objectives for IT value generation (IT vision), and create high-level guidelines for deploying technology-enabled services (IT design principles).
	CBB B3: Strategic Options	Identify challenges and opportunities in the IT function and other business units, where IT can enhance performance. Identify options for action, and evaluate, prioritize, and select these options based on their potential contribution to business value.
	CBB B4: Plan Development	Translate the selected strategic options into an approved strategic plan, encompassing high-level IT goals, programmes, timeframes, manpower planning, skills development, and long-range technology planning. Outline programme ownership, business goals, business value/benefits, and an outline business case at the programme level.
	CBB B5: Tracking and Evaluation	Assess the extent to which strategic targets are being achieved. Review all relevant programmes using qualitative and quantitative measures (such as satisfaction surveys, programme progress, and KPIs), and generate input for strategy reviews.

14.3 SP: UNDERSTANDING MATURITY AND PLANNING IMPROVEMENTS

Recognizing Maturity Excellence

When the Strategic Planning (SP) capability is well-developed or mature:

▸ The IT function effectively contributes to enabling and informing the business strategy.

▸ The IT vision is intrinsic to the business vision.

▸ The strategic plan for technology deployment has the clear objective of supporting the generation of business value.

▸ Strategic planning integrates seamlessly with operational planning.

▸ The IT strategic planning activity is embedded in the roles and responsibilities of dedicated IT and business stakeholders.

▸ Funding of IT strategic planning is recognized as an organization-level responsibility, and budgets are constructed with this in mind.

Addressing Typical Challenges

Some typical challenges that can arise in attempting to develop maturity in the Strategic Planning (SP) capability are set out below.

Challenge	Inadequate engagement of IT leadership and stakeholders on IT strategic planning activities.
Context	IT strategic planning may not be considered a distinct area of activity for the organization. As a result, IT leadership and other stakeholders fail to commit to it, and do not allocate adequate resources, such as time, budget, and personnel.
Action	Advocate among senior management that effective IT strategic planning is a key enabler of business value generation within the organization, and that it is deserving of adequate time, funding, and resourcing.
Challenge	Lack of involvement by relevant business stakeholders in IT strategic planning and priority setting.
Context	Other business units may not know how they can be involved in IT strategic planning.
Action	Raise awareness on how other business units can participate in IT strategic planning activities, to ensure that IT plans and priorities reflect business needs and goals.
Challenge	Ineffective translation of IT strategic goals into actionable projects.
Context	IT strategic goals may not be truly understood or defined in actionable ways that enable them to be successfully achieved.
Action	Encourage development of an actionable project roadmap, with clearly defined deliverables, demonstrating what successful achievement of the IT strategic goals should look like.

Challenge	Programmes in the IT strategic plan are not systematically tracked and evaluated for their delivered value.
Context	Programmes may not be tracked frequently enough to determine whether or not they are achieving the desired objectives or require 'course corrections'.
Action	Promote the ongoing monitoring of programmes for achievement of intended objectives. Incorporate results into the strategy review process.
Challenge	Lack of alignment between IT strategic planning and planning elsewhere in the organization.
Context	The degree of alignment between business and IT plans may depend on the extent to which the IT planners are familiar with wider business strategy plans and vice-versa.
Action	Promote the adoption and implementation approaches that encourage joint evaluation, approval, and sign-off of IT and business strategic plans.

Managing the IT Budget

The **Managing the IT Budget** macro-capability looks at the practices and tools that can be used to establish and control a sustainable economic funding model for IT services and solutions. It comprises the following critical capabilities:

15	Budget Management (BGM)
16	Budget Oversight and Performance Analysis (BOP)
17	Funding and Financing (FF)
18	Portfolio Planning and Prioritization (PPP)

BGM
15. Budget Management

15.1 BGM: OVERVIEW

Goal
The Budget Management (BGM) capability aims to ensure that the allocated IT budgets are spent appropriately and within expectations.

Objectives
▶ Make budget allocation decisions in a deliberative, participatory, and transparent manner.
▶ Achieve predictable IT financial performance by establishing responsible fiscal management and clear lines of accountability.
▶ Maintain the flexibility to respond to short-term challenges and opportunities by allowing managers to reallocate IT funds across budget categories and projects at their discretion.
▶ Make sure that expenditure matches the allocated budget. Identify and plan for any likely overrun in advance.

15.2 BGM: SCOPE

Definition
The Budget Management (BGM) capability is the ability to oversee and adjust the IT budget to ensure that it is spent effectively.

Capability Building Blocks (CBBs)

The Budget Management (BGM) capability comprises the following eight Capability Building Blocks (CBBs), which fall into three categories.

Category	CBB	Definition
Category A: Planning	CBB A1: Budget Scope	Manage the scope and depth of information relating to the categories of expenditure in the IT budget (for example, capital expenses, operations expenses, shadow IT, and so on).
	CBB A2: Budget Processes	Develop processes to manage budget planning and expenditure (such as processes to manage stakeholder involvement, processes to align the budget planning with business planning cycles, processes to manage payments, and so on).
	CBB A3: Business Alignment	Engage stakeholders from the wider business in setting the IT budget to ensure that strategic priorities are reflected in the IT budget priorities.
Category B: Performance Management	CBB B1: Budget Monitoring	Monitor and report to stakeholders on actual performance against planned expenditure.
	CBB B2: Variance Management	Manage deviations of expenditure from the planned budget (by, for example, establishing escalation channels, and taking corrective actions).
	CBB B3: Predictability	Manage IT expenditure within budget targets and variance ranges.
Category C: Governance	CBB C1: Budget Governance	Establish oversight structures and decision rights to set IT budgets and manage allocations.
	CBB C2: Accountability Assignment	Establish accountability for managing the expenditure of IT budgets.

15.3 BGM: UNDERSTANDING MATURITY AND PLANNING IMPROVEMENTS

Recognizing Maturity Excellence

When the Budget Management (BGM) capability is well-developed or mature:

▶ IT budgets are transparently linked to broader strategic priorities and business planning cycles, there is participation by key stakeholders in the budgeting process, and there is budget flexibility that allows the organization to respond to unanticipated opportunities.

▶ The IT budget covers the full scope of IT spending, and forms the basis for monitoring expenditure and taking corrective actions.

▶ Budget expenditure patterns are predictable, and variances are actively managed with well-defined approaches that control cost and risk.

▶ Robust budget oversight and accountability structures are in place.

Addressing Typical Challenges

Some typical challenges that can arise in attempting to develop maturity in the Budget Management (BGM) capability are set out below.

Challenge	Senior management is reluctant to support or approve the proposed IT budget allocations.
Context	Proposed IT budget allocations can often be contentious, especially if allocations are considered ambiguous.
Action	Link the proposed IT budget allocations to strategic business objectives, and demonstrate that IT investments represent good value for money.
Challenge	Significant shadow IT expenditure exists across the organization.
Context	The use of technology across the organization, without the formal approval or control of the IT function, poses risks to data security, IT systems compatibility and/or duplication, as well as impacting IT operational budgets.
Action	Raise awareness amongst senior management of the risks posed by uncontrolled shadow IT. Collaborate with shadow IT proponents to use a coordinated and common approach wherever possible.

Challenge	Inadequate time to fully review IT requirements and the associated costs prior to submission of the IT budget.
Context	A last-minute approach to specifying IT requirements prevails in the rest of the business.
Action	Be proactive and request plans well ahead of budgetary deadlines, giving ample time for business units to accurately prepare IT budget submissions so that they can be analysed, and the viability of shared solutions considered.
Challenge	A general lack of understanding of the business value of IT, with the IT function often being perceived as a cost centre.
Context	The value of IT is not always understood and its benefits are not evident to many employees.
Action	Engage in communication across the business, and inform, in simple and straightforward terms, the business reasons for, and the implications of, IT expenditure.

BOP
16. Budget Oversight and Performance Analysis

16.1 BOP: OVERVIEW

Goal

The Budget Oversight and Performance Analysis (BOP) capability aims to compare actual IT expenditure against planned IT expenditure over extended time periods, and in doing so provides management with the stimulus to confirm or reset budget allocations, where appropriate.

Objectives

- Improve visibility of actual IT expenditure over extended time periods.
- Better inform decisions regarding future funding levels and allocations.
- Improve the quality of future budgets, and identify favourable budget trends and areas of concern.
- Increase confidence that budget allocations can avoid unplanned adjustments midway through a financial cycle.

16.2 BOP: SCOPE

Definition

The Budget Oversight and Performance Analysis (BOP) capability is the ability to compare actual IT expenditure against budgeted IT expenditure over extended time periods. Where appropriate, it offers management the opportunity to reprofile or reprioritize budget forecasts and allocations.

Capability Building Blocks (CBBs)

The Budget Oversight and Performance Analysis (BOP) capability comprises the following seven Capability Building Blocks (CBBs), which fall into three categories.

Category	CBB	Definition
Category A: Analysis	CBB A1: Scope, Granularity, and Sophistication	Establish budget tracking and forecasting approaches (for example, single versus multi-year analysis).
	CBB A2: Tools and Processes	Develop tools and processes to generate budget performance analyses.
	CBB A3: Data Consistency	Develop the sources of data, and structure the data required to conduct budget performance analyses. Develop a common budget management terminology in the organization to enable wider comparisons to be made.
Category B: Impact and Value	CBB B1: Metrics Reporting	Develop a suite of metrics to enable reporting on a range of budget performance criteria (for example, over/under expenditure and expenditure run-rates), and the relationships between them.
	CBB B2: Future IT Expenditure	Inform decision-making for planning of future IT expenditure.
	CBB B3: Management of Unit Costs	Inform decision-making regarding unit cost adjustments – for example, those relating to pricing and consumption.
Category C: Alignment	CBB C1: Awareness and Communication	Communicate IT budget management practices and methods, and details of their business impact to stakeholders.

16.3 BOP: UNDERSTANDING MATURITY AND PLANNING IMPROVEMENTS

Recognizing Maturity Excellence

When the Budget Oversight and Performance Analysis (BOP) capability is well-developed or mature:

▸ The organization has defined and automated approaches that can pull budget expenditure data from coherent up-to-date sources, to analyse and link it to broader organizational activities and metrics.

▸ The organization is able to conduct sophisticated multi-year tracking and trending across the full range of budget categories; and this is likely to lead to improved budget performance, reprioritizing and rebalancing of budgets, more accurate forecasts, and better decisions on consumption of IT resources and services.

Addressing Typical Challenges

Some typical challenges that can arise in attempting to develop maturity in the Budget Oversight and Performance Analysis (BOP) capability are set out below.

Challenge	The IT function resists being measured solely on budget performance.
Context	Management may regard IT budget monitoring as an unnecessary burden.
Action	Promote greater collaboration between general business unit budget managers and those responsible for the management of the IT budget. Facilitate discussions regarding how reporting of the IT budget performance to senior management should occur.
Challenge	Lack of transparency relating to accountability for adhering to planned IT budgets.
Context	IT budget oversight is typically viewed as the exclusive responsibility of a narrow group of people within the IT function.
Action	Link adherence to planned budgets with individual performance management throughout the organization.

Challenge	There is a question mark over the accuracy and integrity of the data quality and performance reporting of the IT budget.
Context	There is a perception that the quality of the IT budget data is not accurate or there are instances where it has been shown to be unreliable. This may lead to resistance regarding any changes to the IT budget, even when there is strong evidence to suggest that it needs to be modified.
Action	Improve the quality and address any misconceptions regarding the quality of the IT budget data. Have open and organization-wide discussions to address when changes to the IT budget are needed. These should be based on criteria other than just data quality, possibly following a weighting system until data quality issues are addressed.
Challenge	Difficulty in making the necessary changes to previously approved IT funding levels and budget category allocations in the middle of the financial year.
Context	IT funding levels and budget category allocations typically use simplistic planning methods (for example, increase or decrease over the previous year) and decisions are typically locked in for each financial planning cycle.
Action	Promote discussion on the need for increased flexibility in cases where resetting IT funding and budget category allocations is required between financial planning milestones.

17. Funding and Financing

17.1 FF: OVERVIEW

Goal

The Funding and Financing (FF) capability aims to generate reliable and flexible sources of funding for an organization, so that it can provide adequate investment and enable the IT function to deliver services and solutions to the organization.

Objectives

▶ Set appropriate funding levels for IT to maximize development of the business capabilities that drive strategic or operational advantage.

▶ Consider alternative sources for technology funding, and understand their associated costs and expected benefits.

▶ Ensure transparent practices and objective governance when agreeing options for funding and financing.

▶ Benchmark IT funding against that of peer organizations to inform funding and financing decisions.

17.2 FF: SCOPE

Definition

The Funding and Financing (FF) capability is the ability to determine the funding level required for IT and to allocate it appropriately.

Capability Building Blocks (CBBs)

The Funding and Financing (FF) capability comprises the following six Capability Building Blocks (CBBs), which fall into two categories.

Category	CBB	Definition
Category A: Process	CBB A1: Funding Sources	Establish sources of IT financing, which may include a centrally allocated IT budget, allocations from other business units, and external sources (for example, joint ventures, industry consortia, vendors, suppliers, clients, and so on). Understand the costs of financing and the expected benefits to be derived from each funding source.
	CBB A2: Funding Levels	Set the overall level of IT funding for the organization based on, for example, strategic priorities and competitive benchmarks.
	CBB A3: Allocation	Allocate funding to broad categories of IT activity (for example, infrastructure/product improvements, capability development) to align with objectives and derive business value.
	CBB A4: Performance Measurement	Use metrics to track, evaluate, and improve funding-related outcomes – for example, cost of funds, spend by category/initiative/business unit, return on investment (ROI), return on assets (ROA), and so on. Link funding to the benefits derived to determine the impact of funding.
Category B: Alignment and Oversight	CBB B1: Governance Model and Alignment	Define guidelines and decision rights for funding governing bodies and promote decision-making alignment with organization-wide decision-making cycles.
	CBB B2: Communication	Discuss funding and financing decisions with stakeholders.

17.3 FF: UNDERSTANDING MATURITY AND PLANNING IMPROVEMENTS

Recognizing Maturity Excellence

When the Funding and Financing (FF) capability is well-developed or mature:

▶ The funding and financing of IT is regarded as a strategic activity.

▶ IT funding and financing decision-making and governance are clear, transparent, and aligned with business priorities.

▶ Funding from multiple internal and external sources is investigated.

▶ The level of funding is adequately set based on aspirations for strategic development, operational excellence, levels of innovation, and comparison with industry benchmarks.

▶ Initial allocations of funding are objectively balanced against operational, business improvement, and innovation priorities.

Addressing Typical Challenges

Some typical challenges that can arise in attempting to develop maturity in the Funding and Financing (FF) capability are set out below.

Challenge	Difficulty in convincing business leaders of the strategic value of increased IT investment.
Context	IT is viewed as a cost centre, with costs to be reduced over time. Typically, there is limited transparency in how IT funding decisions are made, where funds come from, and how they are used.
Action	Clearly communicate funding and financing decisions and underlying rationales to ensure they are transparent to and accepted by relevant stakeholders.
Challenge	IT funding and financing governance oversight is limited to annual budget approval discussions.
Context	There is little appetite for expanding governance beyond initial budget approvals, as this is likely to require more time and administration.
Action	Advocate to senior management the benefits and flexibility to be expected from the continual oversight of funds between approval cycles. These benefits include the ability to reprioritize initial allocations and to adjust funding levels in response to rapidly emerging opportunities and challenges.
Challenge	Difficulty in engaging business leaders in funding allocation decisions, as the technical language used to describe IT projects can be cumbersome and confusing.
Context	There is a general lack of appreciation of how funding of the IT function supports business initiatives.
Action	Using plain, business-level language, highlight the impact that funding of the IT function can have on business initiatives.

PPP
18. Portfolio Planning and Prioritization

18.1 PPP: OVERVIEW

Goal
The Portfolio Planning and Prioritization (PPP) capability aims to establish the investment portfolio composition for technology-related programmes and projects.

Objectives
▶ Increase the likelihood that organizational resources are applied in accordance with the organization's strategy.
▶ Improve consistency and transparency in programme and project selection, based on agreed evaluation and prioritization criteria.
▶ Prioritize technology-related programmes and projects that have the greatest potential for value delivery in alignment with the organization's strategic direction, while managing potential downsides.
▶ Dynamically reprioritize the portfolio based on strategy change – for example, mergers, acquisitions, and business environment changes.
▶ Provide insight into financial, people, and technical resource requirements for execution of the IT investment portfolio.
▶ Improve the perception of IT as a catalyst or enabler of the business, by delivering positive returns on the IT investment portfolio.

18.2 PPP: SCOPE

Definition
The Portfolio Planning and Prioritization (PPP) capability is the ability to select, prioritize, approve, and terminate programmes and projects that are seeking organizational resources.

Capability Building Blocks (CBBs)

The Portfolio Planning and Prioritization (PPP) capability comprises the following four Capability Building Blocks (CBBs), which fall into two categories.

Category	CBB	Definition
Category A: Governance	CBB A1: Prioritization Framework	Use an evaluation framework and a set of criteria to select and prioritize programmes and projects for the portfolio.
	CBB A2: Authority	Involve key personnel in decisions regarding the selection and prioritization of programmes and projects. Approve and terminate the selected programmes and projects as required.
Category B: Process	CBB B1: Assessment and Prioritization	Assess programmes and projects against explicit criteria, such as alignment with strategic vision, business objectives, operational needs, desired portfolio mix and scope, and resource availability. Prioritize programmes and projects based on the assessment results.
	CBB B2: Planning	Develop a high-level plan for aligning the portfolio with the organization's strategy. Acquire information on financial, people, and technical resources to plan their allocation to the portfolio.

18.3 PPP: UNDERSTANDING MATURITY AND PLANNING IMPROVEMENTS

Recognizing Maturity Excellence

When the Portfolio Planning and Prioritization (PPP) capability is well-developed or mature:

▶ Programmes and projects are selected using transparent assessment criteria and a prioritization framework that are continually reviewed and adjusted to provide optimal value to the business.

▶ A central committee, comprising senior management representatives across the organization, is recognized as the sole authority for selecting, prioritizing, approving, and terminating programmes and projects.

▶ The organization's strategic goals are key determinants in defining the portfolio's selection criteria and evaluation framework.

▶ The success (or otherwise) of previous programmes and projects informs decisions regarding the prioritization and approval of similar or related new programmes and projects, and the termination of programmes and projects in progress.

Addressing Typical Challenges

Some typical challenges that can arise in attempting to develop maturity in the Portfolio Planning and Prioritization (PPP) capability are set out below.

Challenge	Lack of senior management support and buy-in for portfolio planning and prioritization activities.
Context	Planning and prioritizing the IT investment portfolio is not perceived as being of strategic importance.
Action	Foster a senior management mind-set in which the selection of appropriate IT programmes and projects is recognized as important to the organization's success, and critical to using the organization's scarce resources effectively.
Challenge	Resources provided for planning and prioritizing programmes and projects are inadequate.
Context	Willingness to invest in portfolio planning and prioritization activities is limited, as this is perceived as an unnecessary and bureaucratic overhead.
Action	Promote dialogue on the merits of portfolio planning and prioritization, and how it should be funded as an important contributor to the realization of the organization's overall goals and objectives.
Challenge	Unwillingness to assign (or accept) responsibility for participating in the portfolio planning, prioritization, and oversight activities.
Context	IT investments are made predominantly based on the siloed interests or agendas of individual business units.
Action	Recognize that assigning responsibility for portfolio planning and prioritization is a way of ensuring that programmes and projects are assessed and prioritized in a consistent and transparent manner, in line with the organization's overall best interests, and that participation in the decision-making process increases stakeholder buy-in to the selected portfolio.
Challenge	Difficulty in reprioritizing the portfolio in response to poor portfolio performance or changes in the business environment.
Context	There is no transparent approach for concluding that legacy programmes or projects are failing, or that they no longer align with the organization's goals.
Action	Stimulate organizational commitment to proactively remaining abreast of business environment changes, reviewing existing programmes and projects, and terminating those that are no longer necessary or fail to meet expectations.
Challenge	Poor understanding of the benefits of effective portfolio planning and prioritization.
Context	The value of systematically optimizing the selection of programmes and projects is poorly communicated.
Action	Promote widespread awareness and visibility among stakeholders on the portfolio's successes and quick wins, and its contribution to overall business value.

Managing the IT Capability

The **Managing the IT Capability** macro-capability provides the IT function with a systematic approach to maintaining existing services and solutions, and for developing new and innovative ones to deliver continual business improvement. It comprises the following critical capabilities:

19	Capability Assessment Management (CAM)
20	Enterprise Architecture Management (EAM)
21	Information Security Management (ISM)
22	Knowledge Asset Management (KAM)
23	People Asset Management (PAM)
24	Personal Data Protection (PDP)
25	Programme and Project Management (PPM)
26	Relationship Management (REM)
27	Research, Development and Engineering (RDE)
28	Service Provisioning (SRP)
29	Solutions Delivery (SD)
30	Supplier Management (SUM)
31	Technical Infrastructure Management (TIM)
32	User Experience Design (UED)
33	User Training Management (UTM)

19.1 CAM: OVERVIEW

Goal

The Capability Assessment Management (CAM) capability aims to provide the organization with an accurate picture of its current IT management capabilities, and to identify areas needing improvement.

Objectives

▶ Improve the organization's ability to identify strengths and weaknesses in key IT capabilities.
▶ Establish a consistent approach to assessing IT capabilities and selecting areas for IT capability improvement that are aligned with the organization's strategic direction.
▶ Identify over-investment in IT capabilities that are of lower strategic importance.
▶ Establish a credible and achievable approach to managing a continual improvement programme, which can be used to verify improvements over time.

19.2 CAM: SCOPE

Definition

The Capability Assessment Management (CAM) capability is the ability of the organization to conduct current state evaluations and plan improvements for its portfolio of IT capabilities. Current state evaluations involve gathering and documenting data about the specific IT capabilities in the organization. The results then inform the planning and execution of improvement actions to deal with any deficiencies.

Capability Building Blocks (CBBs)

The Capability Assessment Management (CAM) capability comprises the following seven Capability Building Blocks (CBBs), which fall into two categories.

Category	CBB	Definition
Category A: Governance	CBB A1: Framework	Determine the capability framework(s) to be used for assessment. Define an integration and mapping approach in cases where a number of frameworks are used simultaneously.
	CBB A2: Commitment	Promote management sponsorship and stakeholder commitment. Provide the required resources for capability assessments.
	CBB A3: Culture	Promote organizational buy-in to targets by, for example, highlighting the reasons for change and identifying the owners of improvement initiatives.
Category B: Process	CBB B1: Assessment Planning	Plan and prepare the approach for conducting capability assessments – examine the organization's needs and business goals, establish assessment objectives, and agree assessment scope, team members, participants, and logistics.
	CBB B2: Assessment Execution	Conduct the assessment, including such activities as running awareness campaigns, employing assessment tools, conducting evaluation interviews, and gathering information about existing practices in the organization.
	CBB B3: Evaluation	Analyse the assessment results, and determine strengths and areas for improvement.
	CBB B4: Target-Setting and Development Roadmap	Identify IT capability areas in need of improvement. Develop plans to close the gap between the current state and the target. Obtain support for implementing improvement initiatives. Communicate with stakeholders about assessment results, targets, gaps, and roadmap progress.

19.3 CAM: UNDERSTANDING MATURITY AND PLANNING IMPROVEMENTS

Recognizing Maturity Excellence

When the Capability Assessment Management (CAM) capability is well-developed or mature:

▶ An integrated and organization-wide continual capability improvement approach is in place, with adequate resourcing.

▶ There is an up-to-date and holistic view of the strengths and weaknesses across the portfolio of IT capabilities.

▶ IT capability targets are aligned with business goals and are informed by industry benchmarks, previous assessment results, and organizational challenges.

▶ Development roadmaps have executive sponsors assigned to them.

▶ Improvement initiatives are consistently prioritized and acted upon. Key areas are regularly re-assessed to check progress.

▶ Stakeholders are sufficiently involved and adequate resources are available to identify and address IT capability deficiencies or gaps.

Addressing Typical Challenges

Some typical challenges that can arise in attempting to develop maturity in the Capability Assessment Management (CAM) capability are set out below.

Challenge	A lack of senior management support and key stakeholder buy-in for capability assessment management.
Context	The senior management team places a low priority on conducting IT capability assessments and identifying areas for improvement. Key stakeholders view capability assessments as having limited credibility and adding little value.
Action	Promote continual IT capability review and improvement to senior management and key stakeholders, emphasizing the value of the activity as a key contributor to the organization's competitiveness.
Challenge	Lack of clarity on the IT capabilities most critical to the organization.
Context	The IT landscape is continually evolving, resulting in a reactionary and short-sighted approach to targeting IT capabilities.
Action	Commit the organization to proactively remaining abreast of technological developments, and to identifying both near- and longer-term IT capabilities that are critical for the organization to succeed.

Challenge	Inadequate financial and stakeholder resources allocated to IT capability assessments and improvement initiatives.
Context	The necessary IT capability improvements identified are difficult to implement because the organization is unable or unwilling to provide the required funds and human resources.
Action	Promote IT capability assessments and the improvement initiatives as enablers of business innovation and differentiation. Position the funding and resourcing of IT capability assessments as part of enabling the organization's IT strategy.
Challenge	Lack of alignment between IT capability targets and business objectives.
Context	IT capability targets are considered in isolation from business objectives.
Action	Stimulate senior management discussion on the importance of IT capabilities supporting the organization's overall strategic direction, and promote greater collaboration between business unit managers when agreeing IT capability targets.
Challenge	Isolated approaches are taken to identifying and prioritizing IT capability improvement initiatives.
Context	Individual improvement initiatives are not coordinated, resulting in conflicts and missed opportunities.
Action	Promote greater discussion and collaboration between business unit managers and key stakeholders to agree the improvement initiatives that contribute most to the achievement of the IT capability targets.
Challenge	Poor understanding of the motivation for IT capability change.
Context	The reasons why change is required and the value expected from implementing IT capability improvement initiatives are poorly communicated to stakeholders.
Action	Promote widespread awareness and visibility among stakeholders of how IT capability improvements will contribute to business success.

EAM
20. Enterprise Architecture Management

20.1 EAM: OVERVIEW

Goal
The Enterprise Architecture Management (EAM) capability aims to deliver an overarching approach within which the IT function can design, deploy, and execute the organization's business strategy.

Objectives
- Enable the IT function to align its strategy with the needs of the business strategy.
- Define the technical standards and operating principles for guiding business solution design and technology choices.
- Ensure consistency and integration across process, information, application, and infrastructure for optimal business performance.
- Reduce business complexity through the reuse and sharing of functional components, and through standardization of technologies and infrastructure.
- Improve business processes and enhance productivity across the organization by unifying and integrating data linkages.
- Promote sound architecture management practices and governance.
- Minimize and manage business, IT, and project-level risks through more informed portfolio and solutions planning.

20.2 EAM: SCOPE

Definition
The Enterprise Architecture Management (EAM) capability is the ability to plan, design, manage, and control the conceptualization of systems, processes, and/or organizations, and the relationships between them. The conceptualization may be layered to represent specific types of relationships – for example, those between applications, business services, internal IT services, security, networking, data storage, and so on.

Capability Building Blocks (CBBs)

The Enterprise Architecture Management (EAM) capability comprises the following nine
Capability Building Blocks (CBBs), which fall into three categories.

Category	CBB	Definition
Category A: Practices	CBB A1: Architecture Framework	Provide the overarching framework of standards, templates, and specifications for organizing and presenting a description of the business and technical architectures.
	CBB A2: Architecture Processes	Provide the methodology to define, develop, and maintain the architecture components, and their interrelationships.
	CBB A3: Architecture Governance	Determine the principles, decision rights, rules, and methods that are used to give direction to and monitor the development of enterprise architecture and its alignment with wider organizational governance.
	CBB A4: Architecture Value	Define, measure, and communicate the business value of enterprise architecture.
Category B: Planning	CBB B1: Architecture Funding	Develop approaches to funding enterprise architecture management and architecture improvement initiatives.
	CBB B2: Architecture Planning	Define the enterprise architecture vision and the implementation roadmap and anticipate business needs and trends.
	CBB B3: Architecture Alignment	Use architecture principles and blueprints to align business needs and IT capabilities. Define the strategy guidelines for selecting IT investments.
Category C: People	CBB C1: Organization Structure and Skills	Define the roles, responsibilities, and skills required for enterprise architecture management.
	CBB C2: Communication and Stakeholder Management	Manage communication with stakeholders who are interested in, or are influenced by, enterprise architecture management, and manage their expectations of what it can deliver.

20.3 EAM: UNDERSTANDING MATURITY AND PLANNING IMPROVEMENTS

Recognizing Maturity Excellence

When the Enterprise Architecture Management (EAM) capability is well-developed or mature:

▶ Enterprise architecture planning is integrated with business planning, and uses approved roadmaps to manage change across the business.

▶ Enterprise architecture artefacts are consistently defined and regularly used by individual programmes.

▶ The development of careers for enterprise architecture practitioners is actively supported.

▶ The value derived from good enterprise architecture practices is measured and recognized by stakeholders.

Addressing Typical Challenges

Some typical challenges that can arise in attempting to develop maturity in the Enterprise Architecture Management (EAM) capability are set out below.

Challenge	Lack of organizational commitment and/or resources for enterprise architecture management.
Context	Enterprise architecture can have difficulty securing adequate organizational commitment and resources due to the supporting nature or role of enterprise architecture within other programmes.
Action	Facilitate discussions on what are adequate levels of commitment and resourcing so that enterprise architecture can more effectively coordinate the transition strategy between current and future state architectures, and can effectively sequence the implementation of IT solutions to achieve the business strategies.
Challenge	Lack of suitably qualified enterprise architects.
Context	The development of enterprise architecture within the organization is hampered by the perception that enterprise architect practitioners have poor career prospects.
Action	Implement a training and mentoring network to help make enterprise architecture an attractive career choice. Enable architects to make good professional and personal choices, and in doing so, increase the level of enterprise architecture expertise across the organization.

Challenge	Lack of understanding regarding the benefits that enterprise architecture management can deliver for the organization.
Context	Management and personnel do not understand how enterprise architecture management can help reduce costs, enhance business opportunities, and deliver on business objectives.
Action	Communicate the value of enterprise architecture to senior management. Demonstrate how enterprise architecture can reduce costs, increase flexibility, and enhance new business opportunities.

ISM

21. Information Security Management

21.1 ISM: OVERVIEW

Goal

The Information Security Management (ISM) capability aims to protect the information held by the organization from damage, to prevent its harmful use (to people or organizations), and to facilitate its legitimate operational and business use.

Objectives

▶ Facilitate information security approaches, policies, and controls, both during normal business operations and in the event of significant information security incidents, to safeguard the organization's information resource's:

- ▶ Integrity (that is, its accuracy and completeness).
- ▶ Confidentiality (that is, its protection from theft or unauthorized disclosure).
- ▶ Accountability (that is, its traceability and authenticity).
- ▶ Usability (that is, its fitness for purpose).
- ▶ Availability (that is, its accessibility and access controls).

▶ Ensure that all information security incidents and suspected security weaknesses are reported through suitable channels, so that they are appropriately investigated and dealt with.

▶ Help employees maintain appropriate levels of awareness and skills to minimize the occurrence and severity of information security incidents.

▶ Provide assurance to stakeholders and regulators that information security approaches, policies, and controls function as intended – that is, they help discover, prevent, and minimize threats and breaches.

▶ Ensure key stakeholders are accepting of the residual risk remaining after the information security technical analysis and mitigation actions for identified security threats have been taken.

21.2 ISM: SCOPE

Definition

The Information Security Management (ISM) capability is the ability to manage approaches, policies, and controls that safeguard the integrity, confidentiality, accessibility, accountability, and usability of digitized information resources.

Capability Building Blocks (CBBs)

The Information Security Management (ISM) capability comprises the following nineteen Capability Building Blocks (CBBs), which fall into five categories.

Category	CBB	Definition
Category A: Governance	CBB A1: Information Security Strategy	Develop, communicate, and support the organization's information security objectives.
	CBB A2: Security Policies and Controls	Establish and maintain security policies and controls, taking into account relevant security standards, regulatory and legislative security requirements, and the organization's security objectives.
	CBB A3: Security Roles, Responsibilities, and Accountabilities	Establish responsibilities and accountabilities for information security roles, and check enforcement.
	CBB A4: Communication and Training	Disseminate security approaches, policies, and other relevant information to develop security awareness and skills.
	CBB A5: Security Performance Reporting	Report on the effectiveness and efficiency of information security policies and activities, and the level of compliance with them.
	CBB A6: Supplier Security	Define security requirements pertaining to the procurement and supply of hardware, software, services, and data.

Category B: Technical Security	CBB B1: Security Architecture	Build security criteria into the design of IT solutions – for example, by defining coding protocols, depth of defence, configuration of security features, and so on.
	CBB B2: IT Component Security	Implement measures to protect all IT components, both physical and virtual, such as client computing devices, servers, networks, storage devices, printers, and smart phones.
	CBB B3: Physical Infrastructure Security	Establish and maintain measures to safeguard the IT physical infrastructure from harm. Threats to be addressed include extremes of temperature, malicious intent, and utility supply disruptions.
Category C: Security Risk Control	CBB C1: Security Threat Profiling	Gather intelligence on IT security threats and vulnerabilities to better understand the IT security threat landscape within which the organization operates – including, for example, the actors, scenarios, and campaigns that might pose a threat.
	CBB C2: Security Risk Assessment	Identify exposures to security-related risks, and quantify their likelihood and potential impact.
	CBB C3: Security Risk Prioritization	Prioritize information security risks and risk handling strategies based on residual risks and the organization's risk appetite.
	CBB C4: Security Risk Handling	Implement strategies for handling information security risk, including risk acceptance, transfer, absorption, and mitigation, as appropriate. Promote interaction with incident management functions.
	CBB C5: Security Risk Monitoring	Manage the on-going efficacy of information security risk handling strategies and control options.
Category D: Security Data Administration	CBB D1: Data Identification and Classification	Define information security classes, and provide guidance on protection and access control appropriate to each class.
	CBB D2: Access Rights Management	Manage user access rights to information throughout its life cycle, including granting, denying, and revoking access privileges.
	CBB D3: Data Life Cycle Management	Provide the security expertise and guidance to ensure that data throughout its life cycle is appropriately available, adequately preserved, and/or destroyed to meet business, regulatory, and/or other security requirements.

| Category E: Business Continuity Management | CBB E1: Business Continuity Planning | Provide stakeholders throughout the organization with security advice to assist in the analysis of incidents and to ensure that data is secure before, during, and after the execution of the business continuity plan. |
| | CBB E2: Incident Management | Manage security-related incidents and near incidents. Develop and train incident response teams to identify and limit exposure, manage communications, and coordinate with regulatory bodies as appropriate. |

21.3 ISM: UNDERSTANDING MATURITY AND PLANNING IMPROVEMENTS

Recognizing Maturity Excellence

When the Information Security Management (ISM) capability is well-developed or mature:

▶ There is awareness and understanding across the organization of the role that effective information security plays in business success – security is recognized as an enabler rather than a disabler.

▶ Business-focused information security measures are defined, monitored, and acted upon by the IT function and the rest of the business.

▶ Senior management's sponsorship of information security is evident, and clear responsibilities are allocated for security activities.

▶ The IT function and other business units agree on the required security levels.

▶ The organization is able to rapidly identify and address new and emerging security risks and threats.

▶ The organization's approach to information security enhances its reputation and builds trust with its customers and business partners.

Addressing Typical Challenges

Some typical challenges that can arise in attempting to develop maturity in the Information Security Management (ISM) capability are set out below.

Challenge	Insufficient resources are available to implement effective information security management.
Context	The return on investment in information security is difficult to calculate, and as a result there may be a reluctance to provide adequate funding for security-related activities.
Action	Consider approaches such as value-at-risk analysis to help justify funding for information security.

Challenge	The level of information security awareness is low among employees.
Context	Information security education and training is rarely given the priority it deserves.
Action	Persuade senior management to encourage employees to comply with the organization's security policies. Conduct information security awareness briefings that highlight the complexity of security threats, their potential impact on the organization, and the measures that can be taken to combat them.
Challenge	Lack of ownership and responsibility for information security across the organization.
Context	IT security management is perceived as not adding value, and as a result the security of the organization's information assets is not actively managed.
Action	Encourage senior management to develop an effective information security governance policy, with clearly defined roles, responsibilities, and accountabilities. Specify audit expectations and remediation actions for non-compliance.

22. Knowledge Asset Management

22.1 KAM: OVERVIEW

Goal
The Knowledge Asset Management (KAM) capability enables employees to capture, share, develop, and leverage their collective knowledge to improve the performance of knowledge-based business activities and decision-making.

Objectives
▸ Get the right knowledge, to the right people, at the right time, and thereby improve the quality of decision-making.
▸ Promote access to formalized documented knowledge and also to tacit, contextual knowledge by facilitating collaboration and communication between employees and, where appropriate, between employees and external experts.
▸ Scan the business environment to identify knowledge that is relevant to the organization.
▸ Organize and index knowledge assets so that they can be easily found and accessed.
▸ Measure the use and impact of knowledge assets for relevant organizational activities including, for example, research and development, operations, and training.

22.2 KAM: SCOPE

Definition
The Knowledge Asset Management (KAM) capability is the ability to identify, capture, profile, classify, store, maintain, protect, and exploit the organization's knowledge assets in pursuit of business outcomes.

Capability Building Blocks (CBBs)

The Knowledge Asset Management (KAM) capability comprises the following eleven Capability Building Blocks (CBBs), which fall into three categories.

Category	CBB	Definition
Category A: Governance	CBB A1: Strategy for Knowledge Asset Management	Develop and communicate knowledge asset management goals and objectives. Develop high-level action plans to implement the strategy.
	CBB A2: Roles and Skills	Determine accountability for knowledge asset management activities, along with requisite employee skills and obligations.
	CBB A3: Value Impact Measurement	Identify and measure the impact of knowledge asset management activities in the organization. Examples include the numbers of new products or services delivered based on knowledge management activities, improvements in existing products or services, ability to identify knowledge activities that support improved decision-making, and so on.
Category B: Structure and Resources	CBB B1: Knowledge Culture	Incentivize a culture in which employees communicate, coordinate, work together, and engage in the creation, use, and sharing of knowledge assets. For example, motivate employees by rewarding innovation and expertise in knowledge asset management activities.
	CBB B2: Enabling Methods	Provide enabling methods (such as tools and techniques) to support the creation, capture, access, and sharing of knowledge assets.
	CBB B3: Knowledge Asset Repository	Design, develop, and adopt a knowledge asset repository (including a defined structure and a method for content representation) to facilitate access to knowledge assets. Record and communicate the location of available knowledge assets.
	CBB B4: Knowledge Domain Experts Register	Capture information about knowledge domain experts to make their areas of expertise and experience discoverable.

Category C: Life Cycle	CBB C1: Identification and Capture	Manage the identification and collection of knowledge assets.
	CBB C2: Profiling and Classification	Manage profiling and classification schemes for knowledge assets and the relationships between them.
	CBB C3: Knowledge Storage Management	Manage policies and procedures for storage media maintenance.
	CBB C4: Knowledge Usage Analytics	Analyse the use of knowledge assets by, for example, user, search terms, and/or knowledge asset category, to improve knowledge asset management activities.

22.3 KAM: UNDERSTANDING MATURITY AND PLANNING IMPROVEMENTS

Recognizing Maturity Excellence

When the Knowledge Asset Management (KAM) capability is well-developed or mature:

▸ It is easier to leverage relevant information, knowledge, and resources (such as ideas, documents, and expertise) to support better and faster decision-making.

▸ Loss of know-how is reduced by capturing both explicit and tacit knowledge.

▸ The organizational culture reinforces knowledge-sharing behaviour.

▸ Knowledge can be readily leveraged by others in similar contexts – those experiencing a problem or challenge that has previously arisen can easily find and tailor the previous solution.

▸ Appropriate roles, responsibilities, and accountabilities for managing knowledge assets are assigned.

▸ Supporting tools and technologies are in place. Knowledge repositories are up to date, relevant, and complete, ensuring timely and continued availability of knowledge.

▸ Employees across the organization collaborate in the creation, use, and sharing of knowledge.

▸ Knowledge is effectively managed throughout the entire knowledge life cycle.

Addressing Typical Challenges

Some typical challenges that can arise in attempting to develop maturity in the Knowledge Asset Management (KAM) capability are set out below.

Challenge	Lack of senior management sponsorship and buy-in to resource a knowledge asset management programme.
Context	Due to the perceived intangibility of knowledge, there can sometimes be a difficulty in articulating the business impact of knowledge asset management activities.
Action	Stimulate senior management discussion on how day-to-day critical business activities depend on the effective sharing and use of knowledge assets.
Challenge	Knowledge asset management programmes can be overwhelmed by complexity.
Context	The cost and scope of knowledge asset management projects are underestimated, and employees with the requisite roles, experience, skills, and accountabilities are not assigned.
Action	Ensure adequate time and resources are given to conducting upfront feasibility studies, to minimize the risks involved, and to act as a basis for allocating resources appropriately and effectively.
Challenge	It can be difficult to foster a knowledge-sharing culture across the organization.
Context	Resistance to the cultural change may be due, in part, to the notion that knowledge is organizational power and that sharing potentially reduces individual power, control, or influence. Additionally, knowledge often depends on inputs and contributions from many parts of the organization, making it difficult to track individual employee contributions. Metrics that focus only on use, without looking at who contributes to the creation and refinement of the knowledge assets, can act as a disincentive to further employee contributions. An overly hierarchical culture can dissuade more junior employees from engaging in knowledge sharing activities.
Action	Incentivize a learning culture in which personal development encourages the sharing of know-how and knowledge. Recognize or reward employees contributing to and sharing knowledge.

23. People Asset Management

23.1 PAM: OVERVIEW

Goal

The People Asset Management (PAM) capability aims to manage the IT workforce's employment life cycle to ensure adequate availability of competent employees.

Objectives

▸ Establish an effective recruitment process that attracts the best qualified candidates.
▸ Identify, manage, and retain talented and high-potential employees.
▸ Incentivize employee productivity, satisfaction, and motivation, and reduce turnover rates.
▸ Link employee compensation and incentives to performance goals.
▸ Promote career development by providing mentoring, training, and education.
▸ Proactively plan for employee succession to provide continuity in key organizational positions.

23.2 PAM: SCOPE

Definition

The People Asset Management (PAM) capability is the ability to meet the organization's requirements for an effective IT workforce.

Capability Building Blocks (CBBs)

The People Asset Management (PAM) capability comprises the following twelve Capability Building Blocks (CBBs), which fall into two categories.

Category	CBB	Definition
Category A: Strategic Workforce Management	CBB A1: IT Workforce Strategy	Define an IT workforce strategy, outlining long-term needs regarding, for example, the quantity, skill level, and geographic location of employees. Communicate strategic decisions to the workforce.
	CBB A2: HR Policies	Draw up and implement HR policies for IT employees, covering topics such as health and safety, annual leave, code of conduct, discipline procedures, workplace diversity, performance evaluation, compensation, hiring, terms and conditions of employment, and so on.
	CBB A3: Job Families and Development Models	Define IT-specific job families and the corresponding skill requirements. Establish IT-specific career development models that outline the career paths open to IT employees.
	CBB A4: Compensation	Establish a compensation, benefits, and incentive system based on job families and the performance evaluation system.
	CBB A5: Culture and Satisfaction	Define and manage the culture of the IT function. Monitor and manage employee job satisfaction, including employee motivation.
Category B: Employment Life Cycle Management	CBB B1: Recruitment	Manage the recruitment of IT employees.
	CBB B2: Deployment	Manage IT employee deployment into specific roles.
	CBB B3: Performance Evaluation	Define and manage the performance evaluation approach.
	CBB B4: Development	Manage training and education programmes, developmental job assignments, mentoring, and coaching.
	CBB B5: Promotion	Define and manage the way in which employees are promoted.
	CBB B6: Succession Planning	Define and implement a succession plan to identify and develop employees capable of filling key organizational positions and maintain continuity. Manage knowledge transfer to support succession planning and prevent knowledge loss in the event of employees leaving.
	CBB B7: Turnover Management	Manage employee exits and post-employment relations.

23.3 PAM: UNDERSTANDING MATURITY AND PLANNING IMPROVEMENTS

Recognizing Maturity Excellence

When the People Asset Management (PAM) capability is well-developed or mature:

▶ The IT workforce strategy is aligned with the organization-wide HR strategy.

▶ The required skilled and competent employees can be effectively recruited.

▶ Job families, career development models, the training catalogue, the compensation system, and the promotion policy are aligned.

▶ Well-functioning approaches are in place to develop and promote employees, including high-potential employees.

▶ IT employee satisfaction is monitored and managed. Appropriate action is taken to improve satisfaction levels, when required.

▶ The organization has the ability to attract and retain the most qualified, high-potential, and high-performing employees.

▶ There are well-functioning approaches for managing employee departures and integrating their successors.

Addressing Typical Challenges

Some typical challenges that can arise in attempting to develop maturity in the People Asset Management (PAM) capability are set out below.

Challenge	Inadequate funding provided to support the management of people and their skills.
Context	The organization is unable to recruit, develop, and retain sufficiently competent IT employees because of budget constraints.
Action	Promote discussion with senior management regarding recruiting, developing, and retaining appropriate IT employees, and how best it can support the organization to remain competitive and innovative.
Challenge	The value of a formal IT workforce strategy and long-term IT workforce planning is underestimated.
Context	A reactionary and short-term view is taken of IT workforce planning requirements.
Action	Stimulate senior management awareness and discussion on the importance of maintaining balanced workforce planning objectives in the short-, medium-, and long-term to support current and future business activities.

Challenge	The skills available in the IT workforce are static and do not evolve rapidly enough over time to support the organization's changing goals and objectives.
Context	The organization does little to encourage employee training and education, and provides little opportunity to engage in developmental job assignments, mentoring, and coaching.
Action	Initiate an awareness campaign, with support from senior management, on the importance of employee career development and advancement. Offer on-the-job support for employees to develop their skills and experience in line with organizational needs.
Challenge	The approach to employee performance evaluation is considered highly subjective.
Context	Compensation systems are not transparently linked to individual, team, and organization-wide performance.
Action	Use objective performance assessments to identify and encourage development of motivated employees and future leaders.
Challenge	Critical knowledge is lost when an employee leaves.
Context	The organization does not engage in succession planning or effective exit management to minimize knowledge loss and disruption.
Action	Raise senior management awareness of the importance of proactively identifying and developing candidates for key positions, so as to provide continuity in the event of employee turnover. Initiate discussions on how best to manage employee exits regarding the retention of critical knowledge.

24. Personal Data Protection

24.1 PDP: OVERVIEW

Goal

The Personal Data Protection (PDP) capability aims to protect personal data from unintended disclosure or use when it is acquired, used, retained, or disposed of.

Objectives

▶ Comply with relevant data protection regulations.
▶ Develop and deploy data protection policies, systems, and controls for appropriate acquisition, use, retention and deletion/erasure of personal data.
▶ Manage timely communication and registration with statutory officers regarding data protection breaches and near incidents.
▶ Verify the effectiveness of data protection policies and controls.
▶ Develop, test, and deploy incident management processes and procedures.

24.2 PDP: SCOPE

Definition

The Personal Data Protection (PDP) capability is the ability to develop, deploy, and implement policies, systems, and controls for processing personal and sensitive personal data relating to living persons in all digital, automated, and manual forms. It ensures that the organization safeguards the right to privacy of individuals whose information it holds, and that the organization uses personal data strictly for legitimate business purposes.

Capability Building Blocks (CBBs)

The Personal Data Protection (PDP) capability comprises the following eleven Capability Building Blocks (CBBs), which fall into three categories.

Category	CBB	Definition
Category A: Management and Oversight	CBB A1: Strategy and Governance	Design, develop, and maintain policies and controls for protecting personal data that comply with relevant regulations and laws, and that align with the organization's business model and objectives.
	CBB A2: Supplier Management	Select suppliers that are committed to observing the organization's personal data protection obligations, and manage supplier compliance with them.
	CBB A3: Monitoring, Reporting, and Enforcement	Establish appropriate measures for monitoring and reporting of non-compliance with personal data protection policies and of the remedial actions taken. Drive improvements based on lessons learned from incidents and near-incidents.
Category B: People	CBB B1: Stakeholder Awareness	Raise awareness of the need to protect personal data. Provide data protection training for employees.
	CBB B2: Data Subject Rights Management	Manage requests by data subjects to access the personal information held by the organization about them. Check that the communications channels and agents are authorized by the data subject.
	CBB B3: Enforcement of Roles, Responsibilities, and Accountabilities	Allocate responsibility and accountability for personal data protection to named individuals, and manage their performance.

Category C: Processing	CBB C1: Security, Access Rights, and Risk Management	Establish, identify, and communicate security criteria, access rights controls (based on life cycle state) and risk criteria for personal data.
	CBB C2: Personal Data Acquisition and Purpose	Develop and implement approaches to obtaining data subjects' consent, giving fair notice, acquiring personal data, and processing personal data fairly.
	CBB C3: Compatibility, Adequacy, and Accuracy	Ensure that personal data is used and disclosed only for the purposes for which it was acquired. Monitor the quality of personal data held, and remedy any quality issues. (The quality standard for personal data is essentially set by the data subject – that is, the data owner. The custodian sets standards and guidelines to help meet the data subject's standards).
	CBB C4: Information Life Cycles	Provide input to information life cycle planning to identify, acquire, process, preserve, and/or destroy personal data to meet business, regulatory, and legal requirements, including those identified in privacy impact assessments.
	CBB C5: Retention and Destruction	Develop and implement controls to verify that personal data is not retained beyond the time specified in retention policies. Destroy data media (all forms – paper, digital, etc.) at the end of the data's life cycle and ensure that obsolete (or deleted) personal data is not inappropriately restored.

24.3 PDP: UNDERSTANDING MATURITY AND PLANNING IMPROVEMENTS

Recognizing Maturity Excellence

When the Personal Data Protection (PDP) capability is well-developed or mature:

▶ The organization understands and proactively addresses the entitlements and rights of those whose personal data it holds in relation to the protection of that data.

▶ Personal data held by the organization is accurate, up-to-date, secure, and accessible only by authorized users.

▶ The organization is able to realize the value of personal data without compromising compliance.

▶ Data protection issues are proactively identified and promptly addressed (transferred, reduced, avoided, or retained).

▶ Customers, suppliers, and employees have high levels of trust that their personal data is managed appropriately.

Addressing Typical Challenges

Some typical challenges that can arise in attempting to develop maturity in the Personal Data Protection (PDP) capability are set out below.

Challenge	Lack of awareness of data protection legislation and the need to safeguard personal data.
Context	Information security and data protection are often considered as one by senior managers. Many managers incorrectly assume that the information gathered is the property of the organization. The extent and magnitude of penalties and related risk exposure could be significant for the organization.
Action	Raise awareness of data protection obligations, risk exposures, and the advantages and value that the effective lawful use of personal data can deliver. Illustrate the relative low cost of compliance (versus potential cost of data privacy breaches). Integrate data privacy actions with the organization's data quality initiatives.
Challenge	Different personal data protection practices in different parts of the organization.
Context	Different parts of the organization (especially if it is operating in multiple jurisdictions) may take their own approaches to protecting the personal data in their custody. This can result in a fragmented set of solutions across the organization, presenting interoperability and integration challenges.
Action	Promote an organization-wide approach that enforces common data protection obligations, while also allowing local needs to be addressed.
Challenge	Funding priorities may mean that personal data protection obligations are inadequately resourced.
Context	The magnitude of fines and risks are often underestimated, and the potential loss of business due to reputational damage is often not appreciated. Decision makers, particularly at board level, may not be aware of their legal obligations.
Action	Use value-at-risk analysis (and similar techniques) to secure commitment to adequate resourcing for data protection.

25. Programme and Project Management

25.1 PPM: OVERVIEW

Goal

The Programme and Project Management (PPM) capability provides a methodical approach to achieving business objectives when planning, executing, and closing programmes and projects.

Objectives

- Increase predictability in programme and project outcomes with respect to schedule, cost, and quality parameters.
- Improve consistency in handling programme and project changes and risks.
- Improve ability to drive strategic change and establish new capabilities in the organization, through effective programme and project delivery.
- Improve business value realization from programmes and projects, with effective utilization of capital investments.

25.2 PPM: SCOPE

Definition

The Programme and Project Management (PPM) capability is the ability to initiate, plan, execute, monitor, control, and close programmes and projects in line with the business objectives, and to manage associated risks, changes, and issues.

Capability Building Blocks (CBBs)

The Programme and Project Management (PPM) capability comprises the following eight Capability Building Blocks (CBBs), which fall into two categories.

Category	CBB	Definition
Category A: Foundation	CBB A1: Governance Structures	Establish a governance framework or approach to support programme/project management decision-making and involvement of stakeholders. Define associated reporting lines, and roles, responsibilities, and accountabilities.
	CBB A2: Processes and Methods	Adopt appropriate methodologies to guide the management of the full programme/project life cycle – that is, initiate, plan, execute, monitor, control, and close.
	CBB A3: Tools and Techniques	Apply tools and techniques to manage individual programme/project activities – for example, risk and issue management, schedule management, budget management, document sharing and collaboration, root cause analysis, and calculating earned value.
	CBB A4: Competences	Define the skills required for various programme and project roles. Develop a training curriculum to support skills development – for example, skills in relation to leadership, stakeholder management, programme and project management approaches, and technologies.
Category B: Control and Evaluation	CBB B1: Performance Management	Define, track, and report on the performance of programmes and projects and on how they are managed.
	CBB B2: Risk Management	Establish an approach to manage programme and project risks, and to monitor their impact on performance.
	CBB B3: Change Management	Establish an approach to manage changes within programmes and projects, and monitor their impact on performance.
	CBB B4: Post-programme and Post-project Learning	Manage lessons learned to improve the execution of future programmes and projects.

25.3 PPM: UNDERSTANDING MATURITY AND PLANNING IMPROVEMENTS

Recognizing Maturity Excellence

When the Programme and Project Management (PPM) capability is well-developed or mature:

▶ Programmes and projects are managed with a business value focus.

▶ An organization-wide or central body (for example, a Project Management Office (PMO)), with clearly defined and documented roles, responsibilities, accountabilities, and reporting lines, is established to support consistency and best practices in programme and project planning, execution, monitoring, and reporting.

▶ Programme and project management methodologies are agile and adaptive to changing business needs, and have the flexibility to incorporate input from relevant business ecosystem partners.

▶ Programme and project risk management and change management approaches are transparent and effective.

▶ Best practices and key lessons learned are always used to optimize the running of future programmes and projects.

Addressing Typical Challenges

Some typical challenges that can arise in attempting to develop maturity in the Programme and Project Management (PPM) capability are set out below.

Challenge	A lack of commitment to developing a good Programme and Project Management (PPM) capability.
Context	Having a formalized approach to programme and project management is perceived as an impediment to agility. The value of having competent project managers, and investing in consistent methodologies, tools and techniques, is subsequently undervalued.
Action	Stimulate a mind-set in which a robust programme and project management approach is viewed as an important contributor to the realization of the organization's overall goals and objectives. Stimulate senior management awareness and discussion on the importance of developing an appropriate organizational structure, competent programme and project managers, and providing appropriate resources and supporting mechanisms to enable timely delivery of programmes and projects.

Challenge	Lack of transparency in programme and project management governance structures.
Context	Decision-making within and across programmes/projects is unclear and impacts delivery.
Action	Promote to the senior management the value of establishing appropriate reporting lines, decision-making processes, roles, responsibilities, and accountabilities within and across programmes/projects.
Challenge	Weak recognition of programme and project management activities.
Context	The value delivered from programme and project management activities is poorly evaluated, reviewed, and communicated.
Action	Promote widespread awareness and visibility among stakeholders on programme and project management successes.

RELATIONSHIP MANAGEMENT
26. Relationship Management

26.1 REM: OVERVIEW

Goal

The Relationship Management (REM) capability aims to ensure that liaison and long-term interaction between the IT function and other business units foster business awareness, mutually align interests, and help minimize issues of conflict.

Objectives

▶ Increase the opportunities for innovation and collaboration by fostering openness and knowledge-sharing between the IT function and other business units.
▶ Use collaborative engagement approaches to guide business units through the technology element of projects.
▶ Overcome internal organizational politics by championing mutual interests.
▶ Earn the IT function a trusted-adviser and honest-broker status with other business units.

26.2 REM: SCOPE

Definition

The Relationship Management (REM) capability is the ability to analyse, plan, maintain, and enhance relationships between the IT function and the rest of the business.

Capability Building Blocks (CBBs)

The Relationship Management (REM) capability comprises the following eight Capability Building Blocks (CBBs), which fall into two categories.

Category	CBB	Definition
Category A: Relationship Management Strategy	CBB A1: Relationship Profiles	Understand the formal and informal networks in the organization and how these can provide insight into relationship characteristics, behaviours, and information flows. This includes an understanding of the organization's structures and culture, its strategic goals, the business models it uses, and the degree of operational autonomy that individual business units have.
	CBB A2: Relationship Management Methodology	Define goals, objectives, and targets for the relationship management function/role. Design the relationship management approach to be taken; this includes details of roles and responsibilities, governance, policies, processes, and tools, and also any required support mechanisms such as skills development.
	CBB A3: Capturing Business Awareness	Design information collation principles so that the IT function can recognize and comprehend relevant changes as they occur in the rest of the business – for example, this could include new business plans or project reports. Identify and develop tools and approaches to support this feedback loop.
	CBB A4: Communication Programme	Design the communication programme to be used to keep stakeholders informed of IT developments, future plans, and other issues – for example, through the use of annual IT reports, IT strategy forums, and IT briefing papers. The frequency of communication is likely to vary depending on issues such as the target audience and message criticality.

Category B: Relationship Management Practice	CBB B1: Advocate IT	Advocate for IT by disseminating information to assist stakeholders (primarily outside the IT function) to understand the role IT currently plays and potentially could play in supporting the organization – for example, demonstrating the value of IT activities and promoting the identification of new opportunities.
	CBB B2: Advocate Business	Collate information to assist stakeholders (primarily inside the IT function) to understand where technology can best contribute to enabling business value and supporting the organization.
	CBB B3: Relationship Prioritization	Prioritize relationships with stakeholders and business units (for example, depending on previous, current, and upcoming business initiatives) to minimize negative impacts of competing priorities.
	CBB B4: Awareness and Responsiveness to Business Intelligence	Maintain awareness of what is happening within relationships to track and act on business intelligence. Route business intelligence (for example, that relating to emerging risks, opportunities, and exceptions) to the attention of appropriate individuals/forums to enable suitable responses.

26.3 REM: UNDERSTANDING MATURITY AND PLANNING IMPROVEMENTS

Recognizing Maturity Excellence

When the Relationship Management (REM) capability is well-developed or mature:

▸ Open and frequent communications help ensure there is a good understanding between the IT function and other business units.

▸ Potentially negative events can be openly discussed in a productive manner between the IT function and other business units (rather than being considered something to be hidden or disregarded).

▸ There is a deep understanding of organizational structures across business units, and this allows key relationships to be systematically identified, developed, and monitored.

▸ Both formal and informal relationships are used to ensure effective communications.

▸ Different communications channels are used as appropriate to the audience and the message being communicated.

Addressing Typical Challenges

Some typical challenges that can arise in attempting to develop maturity in the Relationship Management (REM) capability are set out below.

Challenge	Limited resources and time allocated to develop a proficient Relationship Management (REM) capability.
Context	The IT function is typically consumed by daily fire-fighting of issues, leaving relationship management as a 'nice-to-have' activity.
Action	Leverage influencers within the organization to act as advocates and raise awareness of the importance of having a strong Relationship Management (REM) capability that can help to defuse crises or prevent them from occurring in the first place.
Challenge	Over-emphasis on the formal mapping of the organization's relationship networks.
Context	Putting undue emphasis on these efforts can mean that more subtle connections across the organization are overlooked or even undermined; these include informal networks, hidden information flows, and stakeholders with informal interconnections who span multiple parts of the organization.
Action	View the formal mapping of the organization's structure as a stepping-stone to a more thorough understanding of how information flows throughout the organization and who its key influencers are. It is essential that the map does not drive relationship management, but rather is an ever-changing by-product of developing a clearer understanding of the organization.
Challenge	Only technical competences are valued within the IT function.
Context	The bias towards technical qualifications for IT employees can result in a workforce that is highly skilled in very specific technical domains, but lacks the business skills to communicate the potential value of technical solutions to other business unit audiences.
Action	Broaden the hiring/recruitment and development practices, to ensure that there is a balanced repertoire of skills and competences available within the IT function.
Challenge	The IT function has little influence or input into the strategic business discussions of other business units.
Context	While business users may be invited to partake in management committees of the IT function, there is little or no reciprocation, and IT is not represented in other parts of the organization, particularly at the senior management and C-suite levels.
Action	Actively involve the CIO (supported by his/her direct reports) in informing how IT can support the organization's strategic goals and objectives. Promote the embedding of IT representatives throughout the organization.

Challenge	Organizational politics and 'turf wars' continually undermine relationships between the IT function and other business units.
Context	Friction between business units may originate from a lack of clarity or inconsistencies regarding roles and responsibilities in the management of IT – for example, in governance, role definition, and the scope of responsibility.
Action	Work with senior executives to provide transparency and clarity across the organization about roles and responsibilities for management of IT.

RDE

27.1 RDE: OVERVIEW

Goal

The Research, Development and Engineering (RDE) capability aims to identify new technologies that can deliver business value to the organization.

'New' in this context means things that are new to the organization, including technologies, solutions, and usage models. These could be well established elsewhere (outside the organization) but would be considered new if they had not already been applied within the organization. Of course, 'new' also includes technologies that are universally new or emerging.

Objectives

▸ Identify the promising technologies and usage models that are likely to deliver value.
▸ Limit investments in potentially unpromising technologies through phased investment decisions.
▸ Increase organizational awareness of the accepted approach for identifying and developing new technologies and usage models that are likely to deliver business value.
▸ Manage the pipeline of new technologies and usage models so that business value returns are optimized.

27.2 RDE: SCOPE

Definition

The Research, Development and Engineering (RDE) capability is the ability to investigate, acquire, develop, and evaluate technologies, solutions, and usage models that are new to the organization and might offer value.

Capability Building Blocks (CBBs)

The Research, Development and Engineering (RDE) capability comprises the following eight Capability Building Blocks (CBBs), which fall into three categories.

Category	CBB	Definition
Category A: Alignment	CBB A1: Business Alignment	Align new technology research projects/activities with organizational goals.
	CBB A2: Intelligence Gathering	Identify and categorize information on new technologies and the potential they offer – for example, through competitive analysis, industry networking, and technology scanning activities.
Category B: Process	CBB B1: Governance	Have management and governance approaches in place to align new technology research activities.
	CBB B2: Up-front Analysis	Assess possible new technology research proposals in the light of customer needs, market analysis, financial analysis, and alignment with the technical strategy; and produce a clear product or solution definition that reduces the risk of spending on inappropriate research projects.
	CBB B3: Phased Delivery	Move approved new technology research projects to conclusion through defined project phases such as initial research, prototyping, proof-of-concept testing, and so on.
Category C: Management	CBB C1: Culture	Promote a management culture within which research into new technology is incentivized and can thrive.
	CBB C2: Resource and Portfolio Management	Balance the new technology research portfolio in terms of opportunity, resources, risk, and focus areas to best serve the organization.
	CBB C3: Impact Measurement	Develop methods, tools, and other artefacts to define and apply metrics that can be used to monitor and evaluate the impact and performance of new technology research projects.

27.3 RDE: UNDERSTANDING MATURITY AND PLANNING IMPROVEMENTS

Recognizing Maturity Excellence

When the Research, Development and Engineering (RDE) capability is well-developed or mature:

▶ Resources are used to best effect for investigating new technologies and usage models. This is achieved through the adoption of a 'fail fast/fail cheap' mentality that balances the investment of resources by considering risk and realistic opportunity potential.

▶ A constant pipeline of research project outcomes is produced to enable innovation, solutions delivery, and an enhanced knowledge base.

▶ There is an open, collaborative, and business-aware environment in which investigators have the motivation, time, means, knowledge, and skills to research and develop appropriate projects.

▶ Appropriate business and external partners are actively engaged in research into new technologies.

Addressing Typical Challenges

Some typical challenges that can arise in attempting to develop maturity in the Research, Development and Engineering (RDE) capability are set out below.

Challenge	Lack of constructive collaboration between the IT function and other business units when initiating new technology research projects.
Context	Other business units fail to see the potential value of proposed new technology research projects.
Action	Use business language (as opposed to technical terms) to communicate the potential value to management regarding new technology research projects.
Challenge	Cancelling unpromising new technology research projects at the appropriate time.
Context	Many projects continue past the point when they are no longer viable, due to poor levels of oversight.
Action	Define minimum criteria that a project must meet to progress, and ensure adequate levels of governance are brought to bear.
Challenge	Ambiguous definition of new technology research deliverables.
Context	Definition of deliverables is unclear leading to overspend or time overrun on new technology research projects.
Action	Raise awareness among senior management of the importance of ensuring project deliverables are clearly outlined and documented from the beginning, along with relevant details of resource requirements and timelines.

Challenge	Lack of an isolated environment in which to test new technologies.
Context	Technologies that seem promising, but are as yet unproven within the organization, don't have a suitable technical platform within which they can be field tested. For that reason, they are not investigated further.
Action	Promote the benefits of maintaining a suitable technical environment to enable new technologies to be field-tested.
Challenge	Employee antipathy to submitting of new technology/project proposals.
Context	While employees might have good ideas, they are inhibited from progressing them by a fear-of-failure culture.
Action	Instil a culture that encourages employees to take informed risks, and reward projects that inform learning even if the project fails (as opposed to only rewarding successful technologies).

SRP
28. Service Provisioning

28.1 SRP: OVERVIEW

Goal
The Service Provisioning (SRP) capability aims to identify, deliver, and manage the IT services that enable the organization to meet its defined business objectives.

Objectives
▸ Implement a transparent process for monitoring the services that the IT function provides to its customers in the organization and address any problems as soon as they appear.
▸ Improve IT helpdesk productivity by quickly resolving any requests from customers, preferably during the initial contact with the customer.
▸ Where IT services do fail, restore them as quickly as possible, and plan proactively for any necessary IT service disruptions.
▸ Support business change while maintaining a stable IT service environment.
▸ Promote active stakeholder management of users and customers.
▸ Maintain the services portfolio so that it is fit for purpose and aligned to the organization's objectives.

28.2 SRP: SCOPE

Definition
The Service Provisioning (SRP) capability is the ability to manage the life cycle of IT services to satisfy business requirements. This includes ongoing activities relating to operation, maintenance, and continual service improvement, and also transitional activities relating to the design and introduction of services, their deployment, and their eventual decommissioning.

Capability Building Blocks (CBBs)

The Service Provisioning (SRP) capability comprises the following five Capability Building Blocks (CBBs), which fall into two categories.

Category	CBB	Definition
Category A: Transitional Execution	CBB A1: Service Definition	Identify and describe each IT service offering and its components – these include Service Level Agreements (SLAs), Operational Level Agreements (OLAs), and Underpinning Contracts (UPCs).
	CBB A2: Service Architecture	Define the service architecture and all its component parts, their interrelationships, and the operational processes through which they interface with surrounding processes, supporting activities, and business ecosystem partners.
	CBB A3: IT Service Life Cycle Management	Manage the life cycle flow of each IT service from its introduction through deployment to eventual decommissioning.
Category B: Operational Execution	CBB B1: Customer-Facing Service Operation	Manage customer access to IT assistance – for example, IT helpdesk support, requests for IT services, and IT service performance reporting.
	CBB B2: Internal Service Operation	Manage all non-customer-facing activities relating to IT service operation – for example service request fulfilment, incident/problem management, and service level management.

28.3 SRP: UNDERSTANDING MATURITY AND PLANNING IMPROVEMENTS

Recognizing Maturity Excellence

When the Service Provisioning (SRP) capability is well-developed or mature:

▶ Stakeholders are satisfied with the availability and reliability of IT services.
▶ IT service levels are proactively reported and IT service failures are quickly resolved with minimal business disruption.
▶ IT services, including their key performance indicators (KPIs), are well defined and documented in a services catalogue that is integrated with relevant IT processes.
▶ IT service requirements are regularly reassessed to confirm that they are fit for purpose.
▶ There are appropriate channels for prioritizing IT service change requests based on their business relevance.
▶ IT service management is highly automated.
▶ Customers are aware of the costs relating to their usage of IT services.

Addressing Typical Challenges

Some typical challenges that can arise in attempting to develop maturity in the Service Provisioning (SRP) capability are set out below.

Challenge	Lack of an overall vision or plan for IT services.
Context	The absence of a customer-focused capability to deliver IT services results in unstructured IT activities and poor interactions between IT technical personnel and customers and clients.
Action	In consultation with the rest of the organization, define a service architecture so that the business needs are the driving force in defining the requirements for IT services.
Challenge	Customers are unable to comprehend available IT service offerings, what the services include, their limitations, the associated costs, how to request services, and how to get help to resolve issues.
Context	IT services are poorly catalogued because of inadequate approaches to service identification and documentation.
Action	Work with stakeholders across the organization to emphasize the benefits of using consistent service definition methods to validate the IT services catalogue.
Challenge	Available KPIs don't support objective decision-making regarding goal setting and monitoring of IT services.
Context	There is limited stakeholder enthusiasm for investing time and energy into defining robust customer-centric KPIs to express business value.
Action	Promote senior management discussion on the benefits to having quality KPIs that are relevant and tailored to ensure that IT services are achieving the desired results.
Challenge	A lack of senior management ownership for service provisioning.
Context	Service provisioning is considered a low priority by the senior management team, who regard it as the domain of engineers from the IT function.
Action	Stimulate senior management discussion and raise awareness of how the day-to-day operations of service provisioning are critical to the ability of individuals and the organization to deliver on their commitments, and of how service provisioning should be strategically managed to maximize value.

29. Solutions Delivery

29.1 SD: OVERVIEW

Goal

The Solutions Delivery (SD) capability aims to develop IT solutions that are effective in meeting business needs.

Objectives

▶ Manage business requirements, contain development costs, and reduce the time to market for IT solutions.

▶ Adopt flexible solutions development and delivery methodologies based on the project context – for example, waterfall, agile, or a hybrid of the two.

▶ Ensure that IT solutions follow agreed development methodologies regardless of where they are developed within the organization – within the IT function or within other business units.

▶ Employ built-in assurance mechanisms that enhance the quality of IT solutions to better meet business requirements and service standards.

▶ Design and develop stable and flexible IT solutions that can easily be maintained and updated to meet future demands of the organization.

29.2 SD: SCOPE

Definition

The Solutions Delivery (SD) capability is the ability to design, develop, validate, and deploy IT solutions that effectively address the organization's business requirements and opportunities.

Capability Building Blocks (CBBs)

The Solutions Delivery (SD) capability comprises the following eight Capability Building Blocks (CBBs), which fall into four categories.

Category	CBB	Definition
Category A: Design Phase	CBB A1: Requirements	Manage requirements and their traceability throughout the IT solutions delivery life cycle to serve business needs.
	CBB A2: Design Conceptualization	Apply architecture principles and guidelines to inform the design of IT solutions to meet requirements.
Category B: Develop Phase	CBB B1: Fabricate	Construct IT solutions based on design principles and standards – for example, multi-tier architecture, coding, and security.
	CBB B2: Test	Conduct validation testing to ensure that IT solutions meet specified requirements. This can include unit, integration, system, user acceptance, and regression testing.
Category C: Deploy Phase	CBB C1: Release Management	Manage the deployment of IT solutions into the operational environment.
	CBB C2: Version Control	Manage the control of versions that occur during the solution's delivery life cycle using appropriate methods – for example, methods for initiating, defining, evaluating, and approving/disapproving proposed changes.
Category D: Adoption of Solutions Delivery Metho-dologies	CBB D1: Methods and Practices	Ensure the availability and use of IT solutions delivery methods and practices – for example, requirements management, configuration management, and release management.
	CBB D2: Practice Evolution	Evolve IT solutions delivery approaches and methodologies in response to business needs and in line with industry practices.

29.3 SD: UNDERSTANDING MATURITY AND PLANNING IMPROVEMENTS

Recognizing Maturity Excellence

When the Solutions Delivery (SD) capability is well-developed or mature:

▸ IT solutions are specified, designed, developed, and deployed in a consistent but flexible manner to ensure that cost, scheduling, functionality, and quality are optimized to satisfy business needs.

▸ Solutions delivery methodologies guide the development of technology correctly on the first attempt, keeping errors and unplanned rework to a minimum.

▸ Development of IT solutions is not forced into unsuitable delivery methodologies.

▸ The activities of implementation and testing are performed independently of each other, ensuring solutions are robust and reliable before being released.

Addressing Typical Challenges

Some typical challenges that can arise in attempting to develop maturity in the Solutions Delivery (SD) capability are set out below.

Challenge	IT solutions fail to satisfy users' needs or are considered not fit-for-purpose.
Context	Requirements gathering does not gather input from relevant stakeholders or adequately reflect their inputs.
Action	Raise awareness among senior management of the importance of adopting a robust process for requirements gathering, one in which the needs of all users, from both the IT function and the rest of the business, are gathered and clearly understood.
Challenge	Some of the solutions delivered are not stable, maintainable, or upgradeable.
Context	There are no common design standards in place to provide guidance on issues such as safety and design tolerances; and criteria such as modularity, portability, scalability, maintainability, and organization architecture are not considered in advance.
Action	Highlight to senior management the importance of identifying and agreeing applicable design standards in advance of developing IT solutions.

Challenge	The development and delivery of major IT solutions are often abandoned as management loses confidence midway through the project that it can deliver the desired outcomes.
Context	When a robust solutions delivery process is not considered and agreed in advance, the project is likely to be beset by poor understanding of requirements and ineffective use of resources, leading to a solution that does not address the needs of users, or is terminated before completion.
Action	Stimulate senior management discussion on the importance of a robust solutions delivery process to increase project success rates.
Challenge	Lack of a formal organizational test strategy.
Context	General awareness of the importance of a robust test strategy is often lacking. Some testing may be undertaken but this is often limited to such things as functional testing, and other areas such as user testing are often overlooked.
Action	Initiate an awareness campaign on the importance of adopting a robust test strategy before the IT solution is released.
Challenge	Scope creep and constantly shifting requirements make it more difficult to deliver against defined project objectives.
Context	Scope creep and shifting requirements can often arise from poor change control approaches, from lack of proper initial identification of what is required, from a weak project manager or executive sponsor, or from poor communication between parties.
Action	Stimulate discussion among senior management on the value of adopting a formal version control process across the solutions delivery life cycle and of allocating responsibility for this activity.

SUM

30. Supplier Management

30.1 SUM: OVERVIEW

Goal

The Supplier Management (SUM) capability aims to manage interactions between the IT function and its suppliers.

Objectives

▶ Translate the sourcing strategy into supplier performance objectives and relationship management activities.
▶ Strike an appropriate balance between cost efficiency and supply/service quality.
▶ Foster collaboration, trust, empathy, open communication, and a desire for mutual benefit to encourage co-innovation with preferred suppliers.
▶ Ensure the integrity of supplier performance monitoring.
▶ Identify constraints and scope for manoeuvre when (re)negotiating supplier contracts.
▶ Use suppliers' expertise and innovation to support and inform the IT services' development roadmap.
▶ Engage proactively with suppliers to resolve incidents, problems, or poor performance.
▶ Manage supply risks across the portfolio of suppliers.

30.2 SUM: SCOPE

Definition

The Supplier Management (SUM) capability is the ability of the IT function to manage interactions with its suppliers in line with the sourcing strategy.

Capability Building Blocks (CBBs)

The Supplier Management (SUM) capability comprises the following seven Capability Building Blocks (CBBs), which fall into three categories.

Category	CBB	Definition
Category A: Supplier Alignment	CBB A1: Supplier Engagement	Define and manage the supplier engagement model to be adopted with suppliers.
	CBB A2: Supplier Communications	Plan, manage, and execute the exchange of information that may be useful to both the organization and the supplier.
Category B: Supplier Operations	CBB B1: Order and Fulfilment Management	Manage interactions with suppliers so as to facilitate procurement and service delivery.
	CBB B2: Contract Compliance	Manage the obligations and responsibilities of both parties (as specified in the contract) to avoid or address incidents of non-compliance.
	CBB B3: Supplier Development	Work with suppliers to identify opportunities for mutually beneficial development, such as by adapting processes and products/services, improving performance levels, co-investing in research and development, joint marketing activities, or temporarily exchanging or transferring employees.
Category C: Performance and Risk Monitoring	CBB C1: Continuity of Supply	Manage risks associated with the continuity of supply from external sources.
	CBB C2: Performance Measurement and Monitoring	Manage key performance indicators (KPIs) to inform decision-making in relation to supplier management.

30.3 SUM: UNDERSTANDING MATURITY AND PLANNING IMPROVEMENTS

Recognizing Maturity Excellence

When the Supplier Management (SUM) capability is well-developed or mature:

▶ Relationship objectives and contractual deliverables between the organization and its suppliers are consistently met.

▶ Robust and efficient communication with suppliers ensures that disagreements are resolved through collaborative and creative problem-solving, rather than coercion.

▶ Conflicts and tensions are raised at an early stage, with clear escalation paths (within both organizations) for discussing and resolving them.

▶ Preferred suppliers treat the organization as a priority customer, for example by offering preferential pricing, early exposure to innovative products and services, or ideas to promote continual improvement.

▶ There is a high degree of trust, mutual understanding, empathy, and respect between the organization and its suppliers.

▶ Opportunities for improving the cost-effectiveness and innovation of services delivered by suppliers are regularly explored and progressed.

▶ Risks associated with the continuity and integrity of supply are effectively managed.

Addressing Typical Challenges

Some typical challenges that can arise in attempting to develop maturity in the Supplier Management (SUM) capability are set out below.

Challenge	Relationships with suppliers are primarily adversarial in nature.
Context	An exclusive focus on minimum price delivery can create adversarial relationships, and limit the possibilities for collaboration.
Action	Formalize and communicate guidelines to encourage more open information flow and advocacy between the organization and its suppliers, to promote higher levels of trust and collaboration.
Challenge	Supplier management activities incur high overhead costs.
Context	With a large, heterogeneous supplier base, it can be challenging to monitor performance and remedy underperformance.
Action	Use a central system to hold all suppliers accountable to their individual service level agreements. Such a system enables all parties to view the same data, and facilitates collaborative identification and improvement of problem processes or business activities.

Challenge	One-sided control mechanisms over suppliers creates an atmosphere of mutual distrust and of divergent interests.
Context	Supplier relationships are characterized by measures and controls dominated by the procuring organization, and are not designed to produce mutual benefit.
Action	Discuss with stakeholders the merits of two-way measurement mechanisms and a balanced scorecard to encourage commitment by both parties to agree to shared performance indicators.
Challenge	The organization lacks the skills necessary for managing suppliers.
Context	Supplier management is often assigned to individuals with procurement responsibilities. However, building and managing partnerships often requires different skills from those associated with negotiating price and contracts.
Action	Discuss with stakeholders the need to shift focus from traditional buying practices towards relationship management practices. The shift in focus should be reflected in the time allocated to such activities and in training programmes, and should be integrated into performance appraisals.
Challenge	Inflexible contracts stifle collaboration with and innovation by suppliers.
Context	An over-emphasis on removing ambiguity during contractual negotiations often reduces opportunities for innovation during the contract's lifetime. This results in the supplier's potential to add value being neglected in favour of short-term gains.
Action	Work with stakeholders to ensure contracts allow for supplier performance on non-price differentiators, such as product/service innovation, joint collaboration, or influence on IT service development roadmaps.

TIM
31. Technical Infrastructure Management

31.1 TIM: OVERVIEW

Goal
The Technical Infrastructure Management (TIM) capability aims to holistically manage all physical and virtual components of the IT infrastructure to support the introduction, maintenance, and retirement of IT services.

Objectives
▸ Provide technical infrastructure stability, availability, and reliability through effective operation, maintenance, and retirement of infrastructure components.
▸ Provide technical infrastructure adaptability and flexibility through forward-planning when creating, acquiring, improving, and disposing of infrastructure components.
▸ Provide seamless interoperability across different kinds of infrastructure components.
▸ Protect technical infrastructure and the data that flows through it.
▸ Make provision for effective infrastructure utilization.

31.2 TIM: SCOPE

Definition
The Technical Infrastructure Management (TIM) capability is the ability to manage an organization's IT infrastructure across the complete life cycle of:
▸ Transitional activities including building, deploying, and decommissioning infrastructure.
▸ Operational activities including operation, maintenance, and continual improvement of infrastructure.

Capability Building Blocks (CBBs)

The Technical Infrastructure Management (TIM) capability comprises the following twenty Capability Building Blocks (CBBs), which fall into four categories.

Category	CBB	Definition
Category A: Overarching Activities	CBB A1: IT Operations Management	Manage IT infrastructure activities in support of business activities – for example, the processing, storage, and transmission of data.
	CBB A2: Infrastructure Integration	Develop skills, policies, and approaches to enable the infrastructure to work cohesively as a whole.
	CBB A3: Incident and Problem Management	Implement workarounds, repairs, and root cause analysis (where needed), facilitated by appropriate diagnostic practices.
	CBB A4: Infrastructure Performance Management	Manage infrastructure performance in support of service levels agreements (SLAs) – for example, in relation to availability and response time.
	CBB A5: Asset Management	Manage the deployment and utilization of IT infrastructure assets, including software licenses, networks, physical devices, and virtual devices. Redeploy, retire, and acquire assets as needed.
	CBB A6: Infrastructure Change Management	Manage major technology infrastructure changes – for example, the transition to cloud, major hardware refreshes, firmware upgrading, introduction of a bring-your-own-device policy, and so on.
	CBB A7: Data Centre Environment	Manage all aspects of the data centre environment, including power efficiency and availability, network, cooling, fire-suppression, physical access controls, and security.
	CBB A8: Business Continuity Planning	Manage IT infrastructure to support business continuity planning.
	CBB A9: Configuration Management	Implement overarching policies, approaches, and tools for joined-up configuration management across the IT infrastructure – including, for example, allocation of CPU, memory, and storage to a virtual server, configuration of the laptop build image for a group of end customers, and so on.

Category	CBB	Definition
Category B: Decentralized Infrastructure	CBB B1: Support Infrastructure	Develop overarching approaches and policies for the life cycle management of decentralized infrastructure equipment.
	CBB B2: User, Mobile, and Personal Devices	Implement approaches and policies for the life cycle management of mobile and personal devices.
	CBB B3: Peripherals	Implement approaches and policies for the life cycle management of peripherals and consumables – including, for example, printers, scanners, monitors, and other devices.
	CBB B4: Endpoint Devices	Implement approaches and policies for the life cycle management of endpoint devices – including, for example, thin clients, POS terminals, and so on.
Category C: Communications Infrastructure	CBB C1: Wide Area Networks (WAN)	Develop and implement policies and procedures for the life cycle management of in-house and vendor services and the associated equipment – including for example routers, firewalls, and so on.
	CBB C2: Local Area Networks (LAN)	Develop and implement approaches and policies for the life cycle management of local area networks, including Wi-Fi.
	CBB C3: Voice, Video, and Convergent Services	Develop and implement approaches and policies for the life cycle management of voice, video, and other services where technology convergence is a factor.

Category	CBB	Definition
Category D: Data Centre Services	CBB D1: High Performance, Server, and General Purpose Computing	Develop and implement approaches and policies for the life cycle management of the processing infrastructure.
	CBB D2: Storage	Develop and implement approaches and policies for the life cycle management of storage – including, for example, computer memory, disk drives, solid state disks, and so on.
	CBB D3: Mainframe Computing	Develop and implement approaches and policies for the life cycle management of mainframe computers.
	CBB D4: Infrastructure Related Software	Develop and implement approaches and policies for life cycle management of infrastructure-related software – for example, application integration and middleware software, information management software, storage management software, and IT operations management and security software.

31.3 TIM: UNDERSTANDING MATURITY AND PLANNING IMPROVEMENTS

Recognizing Maturity Excellence

When the Technical Infrastructure Management (TIM) capability is well-developed or mature:

▸ The IT infrastructure delivers and maintains a reliable, secure, and agile environment that can meet the changing needs of the organization.

▸ The IT infrastructure supports innovation and the ability to quickly introduce, test, and try out new applications and new ways of doing business.

▸ The IT infrastructure is cost-effective and can readily scale to meet fluctuating business demands.

Addressing Typical Challenges

Some typical challenges that can arise in attempting to develop maturity in the Technical Infrastructure Management (TIM) capability are set out below.

Challenge	Difficulty in quantifying the business value of IT infrastructure investments can lead to situations where infrastructure investments are inadequate or are made without understanding of the likely consequences.
Context	The benefits of IT infrastructure investments tend to be difficult to quantify. Such investments are often foundational and serve multiple IT services, with the objective of providing flexibility, scalability, or agility for the future.
Action	Encourage investment planners to explore ways of mapping intangible infrastructure benefits to tangible business results. Consider financial modelling techniques such as 'real options' to model the value of future options enabled by infrastructure investments.
Challenge	Lack of suitably trained/qualified IT infrastructure experts.
Context	The organization is not attracting or recruiting suitably qualified IT personnel, or once recruited, they are not receiving adequate training and development to keep abreast of technology changes. The consequence is that the IT infrastructure capability within the organization is hampered by a lack of personnel with the required levels of experience and expertise.
Action	Ensure recruitment targets suitably qualified IT infrastructure experts. Implement a mentoring network and a continuous professional development programme to ensure appropriate technical infrastructure skills are kept up to date.
Challenge	The IT function and the rest of the business are not sufficiently engaged to set priorities for the IT infrastructure planning.
Context	The IT function is not sufficiently connected with the strategic priorities of the organization. This can result in IT infrastructure planning that is not aligned with the objectives of the entire organization.
Action	Have the IT function and the rest of the business jointly plan and set IT infrastructure objectives. This activity can be greatly enhanced when senior representatives from different business units are jointly responsible for planning outcomes.

Challenge	Reduced efficiency of IT operations arising from the need to support a disparate and heterogeneous IT infrastructure.
Context	IT infrastructure environments tend to evolve over time, accumulating an array of different infrastructure components from different vendors – for example, server, storage, network, and purpose-specific support tools. Supporting such a heterogeneous infrastructure environment can be a complex endeavour, can make it difficult to be flexible, and can drive up maintenance and support costs.
Action	Promote management discussion regarding the merits of various strategic options to manage the IT infrastructure – for example, moving to a more homogenous IT environment, finding a solutions provider that can cover multiple technologies, or implementing software-defined infrastructure practices.

UED
32. User Experience Design

32.1 UED: OVERVIEW

Goal
The User Experience Design (UED) capability aims to address both the usability and the usefulness of IT services and solutions across various audiences, purposes, and contexts of use.

▶ Usability relates to the ease with which IT services and solutions can be used from a user's perspective.

▶ Usefulness relates to how well IT services and solutions serve their intended purposes.

Objectives

▶ Shift from technology-centric to user-centric design of IT services and solutions; in other words, make the transition from designing within the engineering boundaries or limitations of the technology to designing IT services and solutions around the needs of those who will use them.

▶ Place the user's experience of the IT service or solution (rather than the service or solution itself) at the centre of design and development – for example, a user's experience of email may rely on computer hardware performance, network connectivity, email client usability, user proficiency, purpose of the task, and the environment/context of access.

▶ Consider users' experiences across their interactions with IT services and solutions – including their knowledge about the range of services available, their experiences of taking delivery of services and using services, the training and support they require or receive, how upgrades are handled, and how redundant services are removed.

▶ Adopt a user experience design approach that reduces development time and cost, and produces IT services and solutions that satisfy both business and user objectives.

32.2 UED: SCOPE

Definition

The User Experience Design (UED) capability is the ability to proactively consider the needs of users at all stages in the life cycle of IT services and solutions.

Capability Building Blocks (CBBs)

The User Experience Design (UED) capability comprises the following five Capability Building Blocks (CBBs), which fall into two categories.

Category	CBB	Definition
Category A: Measuring and Understanding User Experiences	CBB A1: Researching User Experiences	Assess user behaviours, needs, and motivations – for example, through surveys, focus groups, individual interviews, direct observation, and usability testing.
	CBB A2: Communicating User Experiences	Convey user behaviours, needs, and motivations to stakeholders to enable informed action – for example, by using personas, user scenarios, storyboarding, use cases, and storytelling.
Category B: Designing, Testing, and Improving User Experiences	CBB B1: Designing User Experiences	Conceptualize design options for enhancing the user experience of IT services and solutions – using abstraction methods such as drawings, sketches, blueprints, wireframes, prototypes, papers, and formulas.
	CBB B2: Evaluating User Experiences	Apply evaluation methods and criteria to assess user experience of IT services and solutions, and to assess design options relating to them. Evaluation methods might include, for example, surveys, interviews, focus groups, walkthroughs, productivity studies, and usability tests. Evaluation criteria might include, for example, system performance, task success rate, time on task, error rate, and satisfaction ratings.
	CBB B3: Informing User Experience Design	Make available and implement feedback to improve the user experience of design options and IT services and solutions.

32.3 UED: UNDERSTANDING MATURITY AND PLANNING IMPROVEMENTS

Recognizing Maturity Excellence

When the User Experience Design (UED) capability is well-developed or mature:

▶ The organization can consistently design user experiences that successfully balance business, technical, and user needs, reducing the need for re-work post deployment.

▶ The quality of design is continually improved through evaluation and feedback from users.

▶ User experience is continually considered in the development of IT services and solutions throughout their life cycles.

▶ User input informs the acquisition of new technology, and the redevelopment and/or replacement of legacy IT services and solutions.

▶ IT solutions have easy-to-learn and easy-to-use interaction methods, increasing productivity and reducing training needs, and with a focus on eliminating or reducing opportunities for user error.

Addressing Typical Challenges

Some typical challenges that can arise in attempting to develop maturity in the User Experience Design (UED) capability are set out below.

Challenge	Pressure to meet budgets and deadlines often means that user experience is one of the first elements to be sacrificed to deliver an IT solution on time/within budget.
Context	Culturally and politically across the organization, adhering to budget and delivering on time are valued more than delivering a good user experience. This can result in user experience not being addressed prior to the IT solution's release.
Action	Raise with senior management the principle that delivering a good user experience should be regarded as an intrinsic part of any release and should be allowed for in all project timelines. Ensure that those who develop IT solutions are incentivized to take account of user experience metrics.

Challenge	While the IT function invests heavily in developing IT services, the services are generally considered 'clunky' and not user-friendly.
Context	When designing IT services, functional and non-functional requirements are focused on satisfying the objectives of business sponsors, with little consideration given to the users' point of view – for example, users' tasks and goals, and questions such as the following: ▸ How can the design of a service facilitate users' cognitive processes? ▸ What are the users' experience levels with similar services? ▸ How do users think this service should work?
Action	Initiate awareness among developers of the importance of achieving a balance between business objectives and user objectives in the delivery of highly relevant and usable services.
Challenge	A belief that once initial user requirements are captured in the early project phases, there is no further need to engage with users.
Context	Although initial requirements may be documented, there is likely to be ambiguity remaining about what exactly users want, and this can lead to misinterpretation of requirements and a solution that does not satisfy users' needs.
Action	Advocate for methodologies that allow requirements to be clarified as users interact with early prototypes based on the initial requirements gathered (but without encouraging feature creep). This will result in more usable IT solutions that can support better user experiences.
Challenge	Once an IT service or solution is deployed, little attention is paid to whether or not it remains relevant and usable.
Context	Post deployment, little or no resources are invested into understanding how users' experience might degrade as their objectives and work contexts change over time.
Action	Stimulate senior management awareness that understanding the quality of the user experience should not be confined to the development of new IT services and solutions or the upgrading of existing ones. Advocate for a user experience strategy that monitors user experience before, during, and after deployment – to check on the continuing relevance of IT services and solutions for users.

33. User Training Management

33.1 UTM: OVERVIEW

Goal
The User Training Management (UTM) capability aims to ensure that users acquire the skills they need to use business applications and other IT-supported services effectively.

Objectives
▶ Enhance the organization's efficiency and productivity by ensuring users receive the training they need to use business applications and other IT-supported services.
▶ Reduce disruption to the organization's operations due to retraining or upskilling when business applications and other IT-supported services are deployed or upgraded.
▶ Improve user satisfaction levels with business applications and other IT-supported services.
▶ Reduce user support costs in, for example, helpdesk and related areas.

33.2 UTM: SCOPE

Definition
The User Training Management (UTM) capability is the ability to provide training that will improve user proficiency in the use of business applications and other IT-supported services.

Capability Building Blocks (CBBs)

The User Training Management (UTM) capability comprises the following four Capability Building Blocks (CBBs), which fall into two categories.

Category	CBB	Definition
Category A: Development of Training Methodology	CBB A1: Training Resources	Identify resources, including people, processes, and systems that are necessary to meet current and future training requirements.
	CBB A2: Delivery Methods	Identify and employ the training delivery methods that are most likely to achieve the desired levels of user proficiency (for example, face-to-face learning, web-based learning, self-paced learning).
	CBB A3: Training Material Development	Adopt a methodology for developing training content that will meet the requirements of the users and fit the training delivery methods.
Category B: Training Impact Assessment	CBB B1: Impact of Training on User Proficiency and Productivity	Evaluate the impact of training on user proficiency and productivity levels.

33.3 UTM: UNDERSTANDING MATURITY AND PLANNING IMPROVEMENTS

Recognizing Maturity Excellence

When the User Training Management (UTM) capability is well-developed or mature:

▸ Users acquire the skills they need to achieve proficiency in the use of business applications and other IT-supported services.

▸ Training requests are prioritized at an organizational level based on strategic IT development/deployment and business requirements.

▸ Training programmes ensure users have access to appropriate, targeted, and timely content.

Addressing Typical Challenges

Some typical challenges that can arise in attempting to develop maturity in the User Training Management (UTM) capability are set out below.

Challenge	Inadequate understanding of user proficiency needs across the organization.
Context	The focus typically tends to be on ensuring service availability, while little attention is paid to educating users on how they can maximize their use of those services.
Action	Generate awareness of the benefits of having an organization-wide understanding of user proficiency needs, and the contribution that increasing proficiency levels makes to improving both job satisfaction and business productivity.
Challenge	Lack of adequate resources (people, financial, and so on) for training design, development, and delivery.
Context	User training is not regarded as high-priority.
Action	Generate awareness at senior management level of the potential impact on key business performance indicators that raising of user proficiency levels can have.
Challenge	The quality of training across different delivery methods varies considerably.
Context	Training delivery methods tend to be chosen based on localized needs and without adherence to common guidelines. This can result in large variations in the quality of training.
Action	Stimulate discussion with senior management regarding the importance of having guiding principles in place for selecting training delivery methods, so that key factors such as quality, cost, speed of delivery, and access are systematically considered.
Challenge	Poor or limited uptake in the training offered to users.
Context	Users often have diverse preferences for when and how they would like to access training.
Action	Raise awareness at senior management level of the importance of taking users' preferences into account when selecting delivery method(s), and how increased flexibility can improve training uptake.
Challenge	Difficulty in communicating the potential impact of training.
Context	Training is delivered, but little effort is made to assess whether it meets the needs of users and business units, in terms of quality or relevance.
Action	Work with business units to track improvements in user proficiency levels and the effect on key performance indicators.

Managing IT for Business Value

The **Managing IT for Business Value** macro-capability provides a structure within which the IT function provides the rationale for investment in IT and measures the business benefits accruing from it. It comprises the following critical capabilities:

34	Benefits Assessment and Realization (BAR)
35	Portfolio Management (PM)
36	Total Cost of Ownership (TCO)

34. Benefits Assessmer
Realization

34.1 BAR: OVERVIEW

Goal

The Benefits Assessment and Realization (BAR) capability aims to forecast, crystalize, and sustain the business benefits arising from IT-enabled change initiatives.

Objectives

▶ Increase organizational awareness, understanding, and commitment to the importance of creating a value mind-set/culture and sustaining business value from IT-enabled change.

▶ Promote the message that benefits do not come from technology in and of itself, but rather from the change that technology shapes and enables – change that must be led and managed.

▶ Focus management on outcomes of IT-enabled change initiatives and measurable benefits rather than on activities.

▶ Create management approaches to assess potential benefits and likely costs in a transparent and inclusive manner, with a focus on continual learning and improvement.

▶ Define transparent links between IT services and solutions (that is, what is produced or delivered) and their business impact (that is, their expected contribution to business objectives).

▶ Manage organizational interactions across complementary actions, such as process redesign, training, cultural/behavioural change, and incentive structures, to deliver and sustain the business benefits enabled by IT.

▶ Create a common language for describing business benefits arising from technology – for example, achievement of a business result (or end-outcome) that a stakeholder perceives to be of value (which may not necessarily be of financial value).

▶ Broaden employees' focus beyond efficient implementation and operation of technology to include the effective delivery of business benefits from technology implementation and operation across the full life cycle of the investment.

+.2 BAR: SCOPE

Definition
The Benefits Assessment and Realization (BAR) capability is the ability to forecast, realize, and sustain value from IT-enabled change initiatives.

Capability Building Blocks (CBBs)
The Benefits Assessment and Realization (BAR) capability comprises the following thirteen Capability Building Blocks (CBBs), which fall into five categories.

Category	CBB	Definition
Category A: Leadership	CBB A1: Value Culture	Create a shared understanding of what constitutes business value for the organization, and a culture focused on creating and sustaining that value.
	CBB A2: Common Purpose	Create a shared understanding and acceptance of how IT-enabled change programmes contribute to the realization of business value in support of the organization's mission and vision.
Category B: Governance	CBB B1: Life Cycle Governance	Establish governance structures (evaluation, direction, and monitoring) for benefits management throughout the investment life cycle, from decision-making on the initial concept through to the eventual retirement of assets.
	CBB B2: Business Case Objective	Use the business case as an aid to management decision-making throughout the investment life cycle.
	CBB B3: Responsibility and Accountability	Assign individuals who will work to achieve the benefits (responsibility), and assign individuals who will ultimately be answerable for the delivery of benefits (accountability).
	CBB B4: Relevant Metrics	Define and apply metrics that facilitate management oversight of benefits throughout the investment life cycle.
Category C: Benefits Process	CBB C1: Benefits Planning	Identify, map, and communicate the interdependent outcomes that may affect the business benefits arising from IT-enabled change.
	CBB C2: Benefits Enablement	Determine the wider organizational change necessary to realize the intended benefits from IT-enabled change.
	CBB C3: Benefits Review and Harvesting	Establish oversight mechanisms to ensure that the forecasted benefits are delivered, and that the organization avails of any unexpected benefits that arise.

Category D: Management of Change	CBB D1: Behavioural Change	Recognize, accomplish, and sustain the behavioural changes needed to achieve business benefits.
	CBB D2: Stakeholder Engagement	Identify and engage relevant stakeholders to achieve the changes necessary for benefits realization.
	CBB D3: Communication	Communicate the messages needed, and elicit and respond to feedback in order to secure commitment to the benefits realization effort.
Category E: Organizational Learning	CBB E1: Practice Evolution, Innovation, and Sharing	Encourage the adoption and development of benefits management practices.

34.3 BAR: UNDERSTANDING MATURITY AND PLANNING IMPROVEMENTS

Recognizing Maturity Excellence

When the Benefits Assessment and Realization (BAR) capability is well-developed or mature:

▶ There is a shared understanding throughout the organization of how IT-enabled change contributes to the realization of business value.

▶ Stakeholders agree on how to create and sustain business value from IT-enabled change.

▶ A consistent set of benefits management methods and business performance indicators underpins decision-making throughout the investment life cycle.

Addressing Typical Challenges

Some typical challenges that can arise in attempting to develop maturity in the Benefits Assessment and Realization (BAR) capability are set out below.

Challenge	The IT function's culture is focused on technology delivery, with little consideration for the creation of business value.
Context	The IT function may have a legacy role and remit that are limited to technology implementation, and may not appreciate the need for organizational change to harvest the technology's potential benefits.
Action	Promote the principle that value is created by organizational change enabled by technology, rather than by technology itself. Encourage the organization to adopt a culture that is benefits-led rather than just concentrating on technology delivery.

Challenge	There is no common library of business value indicators (KPIs), and this hampers the expression and understanding of how technology expenditure impacts business value.
Context	Different business units measure and report performance in different ways. This makes it difficult for IT-enabled change programmes to express consistently their expected impact on business unit performance.
Action	Ascertain how different business unit leaders measure their operational and strategic performance. Draw up a draft library of business value indicators for review by the business units and agree an approved list. Then require these indicators to be used in all business cases as the basis for how business impact forecasts are expressed.
Challenge	The uptake of benefits management practices across programmes is slow.
Context	Programme managers and stakeholders generally feel that they don't have the necessary time or support to adopt such practices.
Action	Initiate an awareness-raising campaign on the importance of business value management in day-to-day activities. Promote benefits management practices, and regularly check compliance across programmes.
Challenge	Joint ownership for delivering business value from IT-enabled change is not readily accepted by the affected business units. There is difficulty in managing benefits realization because of the cross-functional nature of benefits management.
Context	Other business units may be unwilling to accept joint responsibility for realizing business value if they lack confidence in the programme delivery management, or in the abilities of the IT function or an external service provider.
Action	Work on establishing trust between all parties by seeking to identify and address concerns early in a programme. Consider establishing a joint oversight committee of relevant stakeholders to rapidly troubleshoot issues as they arise.

35. Portfolio Management

35.1 PM: OVERVIEW

Goal

The Portfolio Management (PM) capability aims to monitor and report on the status of an investment portfolio of IT programmes.

Objectives

▶ Monitor ongoing risks, progress deviations, and other factors that might impact on the portfolio's success.

▶ Improve consistency in the evaluation of the portfolio's current status.

▶ Support timely delivery of programmes within the portfolio through effective monitoring of resource allocation and use.

▶ Improve confidence that the programmes in the portfolio remain aligned with the organization's overall strategy and business objectives.

▶ Amplify business value realization across related programmes.

35.2 PM: SCOPE

Definition

The Portfolio Management (PM) capability is the ability to monitor, track, and analyse the programmes in the IT portfolio, and to report on their status.

Capability Building Blocks (CBBs)

The Portfolio Management (PM) capability comprises the following four Capability Building Blocks (CBBs), which fall into two categories.

Category	CBB	Definition
Category A: Appraisal	CBB A1: Progress Monitoring	Monitor and track the progression of programmes within the portfolio.
	CBB A2: Resource Monitoring	Monitor the utilization of financial, technical, and people resources against planned allocations for programmes within the portfolio.
Category B: Sensitivity Analysis and Communication	CBB B1: Impact Modelling and Scenario Analysis	Conduct 'what if' analysis to determine the impact potential scenarios might have on the portfolio's collective resources, schedules, and business value. Monitor corrective actions taken within the portfolio.
	CBB B2: Status Reporting	Report on the current portfolio status, including significant progress deviations, emergent risks, and business value threats.

35.3 PM: UNDERSTANDING MATURITY AND PLANNING IMPROVEMENTS

Recognizing Maturity Excellence

When the Portfolio Management (PM) capability is well-developed or mature:

▸ Systematic approaches are in place for tracking and monitoring programmes within a defined portfolio.

▸ Timely reporting on the portfolio's progress is regularly provided to executive-level management, and when warranted, corrective action can be taken swiftly.

▸ Impact analysis on interdependent programmes is readily available when there are progress deviations.

▸ Resource allocations are monitored for alignment with the organization's overall strategy.

▸ Past portfolio performances help inform how the current portfolio is managed.

Addressing Typical Challenges

Some typical challenges that can arise in attempting to develop maturity in the Portfolio Management (PM) capability are set out below.

Challenge	Lack of senior management support for portfolio management activities.
Context	Portfolio management may not be regarded as being of strategic importance – for example, when scarce resources are exclusively devoted to individual programmes, rather than being considered where they might have the biggest impact across the programme portfolio.
Action	Promote the value of a portfolio approach to senior management as the most efficient and effective approach for deploying the organization's resources.
Challenge	Inadequate investment of resources in portfolio management activities.
Context	Individual business units are reluctant to invest in portfolio management activities, as they view this as a cross-organizational activity that should be centrally coordinated.
Action	Promote the idea that portfolio management will be successful only if individuals and business units across the organization jointly contribute to it.
Challenge	Inadequate visibility of the delivery status of programmes across the portfolio.
Context	Progress, risks, progress deviations, and other metrics in relation to programmes are not adequately tracked owing to fragmented oversight approaches and a reluctance to report activities.
Action	Raise awareness at a senior management level of the importance of portfolio oversight in informing programme reprioritization, and future portfolio planning activities.
Challenge	Inability to reallocate resources between programmes in the portfolio in a timely manner.
Context	There is inadequate utilization monitoring for financial, technical, and people resources across programmes in the portfolio.
Action	Raise awareness at a senior management level of the importance of clear visibility on resources' availability in order to adjust allocation as required, and minimize resource wastage.
Challenge	Failure to adopt a balanced and holistic view of the entire portfolio.
Context	Too much emphasis is placed on individual programmes, rather than optimizing outcomes across the entire portfolio.
Action	Promote to senior management the value of using balanced criteria to evaluate the entire portfolio – where such criteria encompass the organization's strategic direction and business objectives.

Challenge	Poor organizational awareness of the benefits from portfolio management activities.
Context	Portfolio management activities are poorly monitored and communicated.
Action	Promote widespread awareness among stakeholders of successes and quick wins arising from portfolio management activities.

TCO

36. Total Cost of Ownership

36.1 TCO: OVERVIEW

Goal

The Total Cost of Ownership (TCO) capability aims to collect, analyse, and disseminate data on all costs associated with an IT asset or IT-enabled business service throughout its life cycle, from initial acquisition, through deployment, operations, and maintenance, to its eventual removal.

Objectives

▸ Establish a standardized method of estimating, tracking, comparing, and managing the life cycle costs of IT assets and IT-enabled business services.

▸ Improve IT investment decisions by systematically comparing the incremental costs (direct and indirect) of competing systems to the full costs of existing systems.

▸ Raise awareness in the organization of the full costs of IT, and promote strategic budgeting by collecting and disseminating data on the full life cycle costs of technology.

▸ Improve the accuracy of total cost of ownership forecasts based on lessons learned from comparing forecasted and actual costs incurred.

36.2 TCO: SCOPE

Definition

The Total Cost of Ownership (TCO) capability is the ability to identify, compare, and control all direct and indirect costs associated with IT assets and IT-enabled business services.

Capability Building Blocks (CBBs)

The Total Cost of Ownership (TCO) capability comprises the following seven Capability Building Blocks (CBBs), which fall into three categories.

Category	CBB	Definition
Category A: Models, Tools, and Methods	CBB A1: Cost Coverage	Identify cost drivers throughout the life cycle of the asset or IT-enabled business service, to include direct and indirect costs involved in acquisition, operations, enhancements, and end of life.
	CBB A2: Tracking Methods	Establish methods to track total cost of ownership, and integrate them into the financial accounting systems of the organization.
	CBB A3: Data Reliability	Create reliable total cost of ownership analysis for IT assets and IT-enabled business services.
Category B: Adoption and Impact	CBB B1: Adoption	Promote organizational uptake of total cost of ownership models, tools, and methods.
	CBB B2: Impact on Decision-Making	Use total cost of ownership data to inform business decisions, such as decisions to invest in, retire or replace systems, and also decisions relating to budget planning, and evaluation of competing options and business cases.
Category C: Stakeholder Management	CBB C1: Communication	Communicate total cost of ownership activities and outcomes with key stakeholders.
	CBB C2: Inclusion	Involve stakeholders in relevant total cost of ownership calculation decisions to support the financial management of IT.

36.3 TCO: UNDERSTANDING MATURITY AND PLANNING IMPROVEMENTS

Recognizing Maturity Excellence

When the Total Cost of Ownership (TCO) capability is well-developed or mature:

▶ The organization is able to identify opportunities for reducing costs by reliably tracking the total cost of ownership across all classes of IT assets and IT-enabled business services.

▶ Total cost of ownership models incorporate a comprehensive set of direct and indirect costs, and are continually refreshed based on actual costs realized.

▶ Strategic portfolio decisions, including investment and retirement decisions, are better informed.

▶ The total cost of ownership approach is fully aligned with the wider organizational finance systems and IT asset and software licensing databases for costs and asset tracking.

▶ Total cost of ownership methods are clear and transparent. Decisions based on total cost of ownership also consider business benefits and are made jointly with relevant business stakeholders.

Addressing Typical Challenges

Some typical challenges that can arise in attempting to develop maturity in the Total Cost of Ownership (TCO) capability are set out below.

Challenge	Concerns that additional overheads may be associated with total cost of ownership activities.
Context	Although likely to reduce long-term costs, total cost of ownership modelling itself initially adds cost by gathering and considering more information.
Action	Engage leaders in simplifying the tracking of total cost of ownership.
Challenge	Lack of belief in the benefits associated with total cost of ownership activities.
Context	Collecting accurate total cost of ownership data can be cost prohibitive if such data is fragmented across the organization.
Action	Use any cost data available, including that from industry peers and vendors, to estimate rough cost models and to identify quick wins.
Challenge	Stakeholder commitment to achieving cost management goals wanes after initial successes.
Context	Organizational fatigue prevails following initial achievements, leading to a failure to identify new opportunities to challenge cost drivers.
Action	Continually promote recent case studies and the benefits of understanding total cost of ownership across the organization.

C. Going forward with IT-CMF

Next Steps

The Innovation Value Institute has a dual mandate – facilitating the ongoing development of IT-CMF, and promoting its adoption globally. IT-CMF is a flexible and adaptable framework that can be used in a variety of ways by different organizations to improve their IT capabilities, depending on their situation and their ambitions. The Institute has developed a range of enabling structures and artefacts to help organizations maximize their benefit from using the framework; these are accessible via the IVI licensed user portal. These structures and artefacts have been tried and tested in a variety of environments, and so they work as design patterns that enable any organization to deploy them with confidence, instead of trying to reinvent their own individual approaches. In developing these supports, IVI recognizes that organizations require a solution template to improve their capability, but that it must be sufficiently flexible and adaptable to be useful in each individual context; IVI's Capability Improvement Programme (CIP) is one such solution template (methodology).

Some of the ways in which organizations typically use IT-CMF include:
- IT-CMF assessment and benchmarking.
- IT-CMF Critical Capability mapping onto the IT operating model.
- IT-CMF Critical Capability mapping onto management roles.
- IT-CMF mapping to incumbent/legacy frameworks.
- IT-CMF as a platform for targeting IT and business problems/opportunities.
- IT-CMF as a platform for employee training and skills development.

These are described below. In all instances, we recommend that an organization considering adopting IT-CMF should engage with IVI or with one of its certified partners, so that their individual needs can be assessed, and IT-CMF can be applied optimally to drive increased levels of agility, innovation, and value for the organization. Contact details are available via the website: www.ivi.ie/partners.

IVI's certified international partner network is growing steadily. The Institute has trained and certified thousands of professional service providers, educational institutions, and training organizations who provide competence services associated with IT-CMF. If you are interested in joining this network, please contact IVI via the website: www.ivi.ie/contact.

IT-CMF Assessment and Benchmarking

A core function of IT-CMF is to provide an assessment (or reference) framework along with associated improvement roadmaps to help an organization continually manage and develop the IT capability in support of agility, innovation, and value. Assessment can range from the formal – where IT-CMF is used by a certified third-party to audit the organization, to the informal – where IT-CMF guides general management discussion. As IT-CMF is a cross-industry approach, it can be supplemented with benchmarking insights from peer organizations. Capability maturity comparisons with industry peer groups can prove very informative.

When more granular insights on a Critical Capability are sought, an organization should consider a 'deep-dive' assessment with IVI or with one of its certified partners, in which a Critical Capability's context and complexity are examined in more detail. (See Appendix 1 for a list of available formal assessments).

IT-CMF Critical Capability Mapping onto the IT Operating Model

An IT operating model defines how the critical work of the IT function is carried out. By mapping IT-CMF's Critical Capabilities onto the IT function's operating model, the operating model is clarified, and the actions needed to drive continual improvement can be more easily identified and ownership assigned. Similarly, IT-CMF's Critical Capabilities can be mapped onto the organization's IT value chain.

IT-CMF Critical Capability Mapping onto Management Roles

IT-CMF can be used to assign executive sponsorship for developing each of the Critical Capabilities that are key to success for the organization, and a framework for assessing performance and progress. This ensures that there is clear ownership and accountability for the ongoing development of Critical Capabilities, and also helps to identify overlapping responsibilities and gaps in the responsibility and accountability coverage for Critical Capabilities.

IT-CMF Mapping to Incumbent or Legacy Frameworks

Organizations can use IT-CMF as a strategic umbrella framework, allowing discrete IT management frameworks and approaches already in use within the organization for specific areas to be used in a unified manner, integrating and filling gaps between such approaches. IT-CMF provides the holistic view that systematically identifies weaknesses in the value delivery chain, and helps derive improvement plans.

IT-CMF as a Platform for Targeting IT and Business Problems/Opportunities

IT-CMF's Critical Capabilities can be combined and configured to target specific challenges and opportunities in the IT function and in the wider business, such as high costs, limited innovation, the adoption of emerging technologies, and so on. IVI is continually working to determine the combinations of Critical Capabilities that are particularly applicable to specific types of problems and opportunities.

IT-CMF as a Platform for Employee Training and Skills Development

IT-CMF's Critical Capabilities represent organization-level behaviours and outcomes. Once the organization has agreed the Critical Capabilities that it wishes to develop, it can quickly deduce its human resource needs and prioritize the development of the employee competences that are needed to enhance and sustain organization-level behaviours and outcomes.

Organizations using IT-CMF can avail of IVI's certified Capability Improvement Programme[1] – in which all the enabling tools, training, and artefacts are integrated for seamless execution. This programme is available through multiple channels, including online and through IVI's certified international partner network. In addition, IVI has a comprehensive suite of training offerings, ranging from executive overviews to in-depth topic-specific courses. It also offers formal academic education courses, including a university master's degree. These training and education offerings are designed for managers, practitioners, consultants, and academics. (See Appendix 2 for a list of available training programmes).

Continuous Development of IT-CMF and IVI

The growth and reach of IVI in the development and promotion of IT-CMF continues at an accelerated pace. Ongoing development of IT-CMF has remained critical to ensuring its currency and relevance to a growing ecosystem. As technology continues to evolve, and as academic researchers and industry practitioners continue to develop and share new practices for the management of IT, IT-CMF continues to be developed as a living body of knowledge. While this book presents a guide to IT-CMF's body of knowledge as it is today, new practices and learnings are continually added to the body of knowledge upon which IT-CMF is based.

One of the strengths of IT-CMF is the user community that has grown up around it. IVI's member organizations and users continually share their experiences of using IT-CMF and of the particular challenges they face in their day-to-day work. This results in continual re-evaluation and refinement of the framework and the various elements within it, so that it is constantly relevant and useful. The latest developments are always published on IVI's website: www.ivi.ie. The website also has more information on the background and history of IT-CMF, and additional tools, tips, and templates to assist in its effective deployment.

IVI has attracted a community of users who are committed to improving their management of technology. It includes many of the world's leading organizations and academic institutions who openly share information, insights, lessons learned, and challenges faced, so that all can benefit. You are welcome to join in this exciting, challenging, and rewarding work.

---

[1]See Capability Improvement Programme on pp. 13–18

Similarly, if you have any questions about IT-CMF or about how it might be applied in your organization, contact us at IVI. We also welcome any comments on this book or suggestions for improvement in future editions.

To get involved, email ivi@nuim.ie, visit www.ivi.ie, or call IVI on +353 (0)1 708 6931.

D. Appendices

IVI Assessments 1

IVI assessments are pre-configured and available online through the IVI portal for consortium members, licensed users, and partners. It is recommended that formal assessments are completed by IVI trained and certified assessors.

The purpose of assessment is to identify and prioritize an organization's or team's performance improvement priorities to help ensure that they can meet their target business goals. This is achieved through an online survey followed by key stakeholder interviews or workshops to validate and elaborate the survey findings. An assessment report will normally include currently assessed performance and/or maturity levels for each question domain. It will also identify what participants view as the most important areas for improvement, along with what they believe the improvement target should be. The results can be benchmarked internally in an organization or across similar organizations drawn from IVI's confidential, anonymized benchmark database.

The available assessments are described below.

Digital Readiness Assessment

The purpose of the Digital Readiness Assessment is to support an organization or team in the identification of what Critical Capabilities and improvements are required to support their digital agenda or transformation goals. The focus of this assessment is:

- The current scale of the organization's digital transformation (i.e. its breadth or reach of digitalization) and its future ambition.
- The current scope of the organization's digital transformation (i.e. the intensity of digitalization across the business) and its future ambition.
- The organization's digital technology adoption trends.
- The organization's drivers for digital transformation.
- The organization's barriers to digital transformation.
- The focus area of the organization's digital transformation strategy (i.e. customer engagement, digitized products and services, or operational excellence).
- The organization's digital business behaviour levels and priorities, detailing the organization's current and future ambition level of achievement across 40 digital behaviours, grouped into seven themes.

▶ The priority Critical Capabilities that require improvement to help the organization achieve its digital agenda.

Cloud Adoption Assessment

The purpose of the Cloud Adoption Assessment is to support an organization or team in the identification of the Critical Capabilities and improvements required to develop and implement cloud technologies and services to support their overall business aims. The focus of this assessment is:

▶ Cloud strategic intent, including drivers, strategy, and vendor selection.
▶ Cloud critical success factors and supporting CCs: strategic planning, governance and alignment, security, regulatory and legal compliance, data management and protection, service management, total cost of ownership, supplier selection and governance, interoperability and integration, agility, and the changing role of IT.
▶ Cloud impact: penetration and benefits.

Data Protection (Privacy) Assessment

The purpose of the Data Protection (Privacy) assessment is to help an organization identify the Capability Building Blocks that need to be put in place or improved to ensure that it can effectively manage personal data in compliance with good practice and with data protection regulations. The assessment will help an organization to:

▶ Understand the extent to which policies and controls for protecting personal data are adhered to.
▶ Identify and apply relevant data protection regulations and standards.
▶ Manage data protection relationships and agreements with third parties.
▶ Understand the effectiveness of access right controls for personal data protection.
▶ Manage data privacy risks.
▶ Manage data subject rights.
▶ Maintain the quality and integrity of personal data.
▶ Process personal data throughout its life cycle in line with intended purposes.
▶ Verify the effectiveness of data protection policies, and report instances of non-compliance.

IT Effectiveness Assessment

The purpose of the IT Effectiveness Assessment is to help an organization examine its overall capability maturity level across all of the 36 Critical Capabilities that underpin the performance of IT – in supporting business needs and in providing the operational backbone that underpins its digital agenda. For each Critical Capability, it measures the current level of maturity and identifies the improvements gap that needs to be bridged to reach the desired maturity level.

Services Management Capability Assessment

The purpose of the Services Management Capability Assessment is to help an organization to focus on 'the bigger picture' of strategic business alignment in services management. It is based on the international standard ISO/IEC 20000-1:2011 and is integrated with ITIL:2011. The assessment will help an organization to:

▶ Focus on the management of its IT service and operational capabilities.
▶ Review its services management functions in the context of delivering business value.
▶ Understand its capability maturity across all aspects of the organization's services management.
▶ Understand how to prioritize and improve critical IT-related capabilities in order to increase the value realised from IT.
▶ Adopt a forward thinking approach and position services management functions as valued business partners.

Individual Critical Capability Assessments

Individual Critical Capability assessments are available for each of the 36 Critical Capabilities. These assessments involve an in-depth examination of the maturity level of each of the Capability Building Blocks that are the key components of that Critical Capability. The outcome consists of recommendations for improvements in practice to reach target maturity in priority Capability Building Blocks.

IT Priorities (Triage-Accelerator)

The IT Priorities (Triage-Accelerator) assessment is a high-level assessment whose purpose is to enable a dialogue between IT and the business to help determine what are the IT priorities and what are the areas that require improvement in order to meet business needs. This is a short assessment in which the same questions are posed to stakeholders from IT and from the business, in technical and in non-technical terms as appropriate. This assessment focuses on the top ten business issues faced by most organizations, and in each case it identifies:

▶ The value propositions associated with the issue.
▶ The *anchor* Critical Capability to deliver the value propositions.
▶ The *core* and *supporting* Critical Capabilities that can make a contribution.

Informal Assessments

Though the formal assessment questions are only available through the IVI portal to licensed users, sample questions and question domains are available to anyone who has access to *IT Capability Maturity Framework: The Body of Knowledge Guide* (2nd edition, 2016). In meeting or workshop formats, individuals and teams can use the body of knowledge to look at specific Critical Capabilities or groups of Critical Capabilities, and quickly review, analyse, and discuss opportunities for improvement using the available information and references.

IVI Training Programmes 2

IT-CMF Passport (1-day class or 6 hours e-learning)

This course is an introduction to the fundamental principles of IT-CMF, including basic concepts, framework hierarchy and structure, capability maturity curve, and the assessment process. An understanding of the framework's fundamentals is essential for the implementation of IT-CMF to improve IT capability maturity.

IT-CMF Core (3-day class)

This course expands participants' knowledge of IT-CMF, and shows how to use IT-CMF artefacts to improve IT capability maturity in their organizations. A comprehensive understanding of the framework and the skills to apply it are essential to use IT-CMF and to implement a capability improvement programme.

IT-CMF Core CC Elective Modules

(Half-day class per elective CC as part of the IT-CMF Core course)

As part of the IT-CMF Core training programme, participants can choose two Critical Capabilities to explore in detail as worked examples. Typically, these are CCs that are key areas of interest to the participants and relate to how they plan to use IT-CMF to improve capability maturity in their organizations. Each CC elective includes two modules and two exercises. The modules cover the selected CC and a sample CC Assessment Report in detail; the associated exercises build the knowledge and skills required to use the CC's Practices-Outcomes-Metrics (POMs) to design a capability improvement plan. IVI currently offers CC elective modules for the most in-demand CCs.

Conducting IT-CMF Assessments for Consultants (4-day class)

This course is an accelerated path to competency for consultants developing the knowledge and skills required to conduct IT Effectiveness and Critical Capability assessments and to lead capability improvement programmes for their clients.

Conducting IT Effectiveness Assessments (2-day class)

This course is designed to enable participants to conduct IT Effectiveness assessments independently. The programme is a path to competency for consultants and end-users (including capability improvement teams) to developing the knowledge and skills required to manage this IT-CMF assessment type. Participants will be qualified to independently manage an IT Effectiveness assessment for their clients or within their own organizations.

Conducting Digital Readiness Assessments (2-day class)

This course is designed to enable participants to conduct IT-CMF Digital Readiness assessments independently. It is a path to competency for consultants and end-users (including capability improvement teams) to developing the knowledge and skills required to manage this IT-CMF assessment type. Participants will be qualified to independently manage Digital Readiness assessments for their clients or within their own organizations.

Conducting Cloud Adoption Assessments (2-day class)

This course is designed to enable participants to conduct IT-CMF Cloud Adoption assessments independently. It is a path to competency for consultants and end-users (including capability improvement teams) to developing the knowledge and skills required to manage this IT-CMF assessment type. Participants will be qualified to independently manage Cloud Adoption assessments for their clients or within their own organizations.

Conducting IT-CMF Critical Capability Assessments (3-day class)

This course is designed to enable organizations using IT-CMF to conduct IT-CMF Critical Capability assessments independently. The programme is a path to competency for end-users (including capability improvement teams) to developing the knowledge and skills required to manage this IT-CMF assessment type. Participants will be qualified to independently manage an IT-CMF Critical Capability assessment within their own organizations.

Capability Improvement Programme Workshop (1-day class)

This workshop is designed to enable organizations already familiar with IT-CMF to use the artefacts and IVI's capability improvement method to run capability improvement programmes. The content of this workshop is integral to the Conducting IT-CMF Assessments for Consultants course. When delivered as a stand-alone workshop, it is not formally certified.

(Note: Where an IT professional has completed a 2, 3, or 4-day Conducting an Assessment Course, a shorter incremental training course can be taken to add additional assessment types).

Capability Performance Indicators 3

Each of the Critical Capabilities within IT-CMF has a range of Capability Performance Indicators (CPIs) that practitioners can apply in the development of capability maturity.

The CPIs for each Critical Capability are listed below, grouped in the four balanced scorecard segments: **Financial, Processes, Learning and Growth,** and **Customer.**

Licensed users of IT-CMF can access the full details and formulae for all CPIs online on the IVI Digital Platform.

01: ACCOUNTING AND ALLOCATION (AA)

Balanced Scorecard Segment	Capability Performance Indicators
Financial	Average cost of generating chargeback/show-back per service
	Percentage of IT costs charged back to the business
	IT service costs per user
Processes	Percentage of business units with involvement in cost allocation
	Percentage of IT services with cost allocation reporting
	Service asset costs included in the cost model
	Percentage of services with benchmarked cost models
	Percentage of financial data collected from a single unified source
	Percentage of services with demand driven pricing
	Percentage of services that offer flexibility of service configuration

Balanced Scorecard Segment	Capability Performance Indicators
Learning and Growth	Percentage of cost reductions in response to cost allocation data
	Percentage of assets reassigned or decommissioned in response to cost allocation data
	Opportunity costs of service spend
	Level of support for cost reduction
Customer	Manager satisfaction with cost allocation equitability across business units
	Manager satisfaction with service alternatives
	Manager satisfaction with business/IT engagement for cost allocation
	Percentage of IT services with differentiated prices
	Stakeholder satisfaction with chargeback/show-back invoice clarity
	Stakeholder satisfaction with pricing model clarity

02: BUSINESS PLANNING (BP)

Balanced Scorecard Segment	Capability Performance Indicators
Financial	IT annual budget
	IT budgetary resources available for investment
	IT budget spend on initiatives identified by the IT business plan
Processes	Effectiveness of the IT business plan
	Time to create the IT business plan
	Percentage of IT business plan deliverables aligned with IT strategic objectives
	Ratio of planned vs. actual deliverables
Learning and Growth	Percentage of IT business planning process improvements implemented
	Number of documented learnings from IT business plan process reviews
	Stakeholder ownership of critical success factors
Customer	Stakeholder involvement in IT business planning activities
	Stakeholder satisfaction with the IT business plan
	Stakeholder awareness of the content/deliverables of the IT business plan

03: BUSINESS PROCESS MANAGEMENT (BPM)

Balanced Scorecard Segment	Capability Performance Indicators
Financial	Cost of process incidents
	Financial impact of process automation
	Cost benefit analysis of process management
Processes	Percentage of business processes documented end-to-end
	Percentage of key processes with clearly identifiable owners
	Percentage of business processes in compliance with standards
Learning and Growth	Percentage of business process personnel with BPM certifications/qualifications
	Business process maturity
	Percentage of employees with business process training
	Percentage of projects that assess the impact of process changes
Customer	Stakeholder satisfaction with business process improvements
	Actual vs. forecasted benefits from process improvements

04: CAPACITY FORECASTING AND PLANNING (CFP)

Balanced Scorecard Segment	Capability Performance Indicators
Financial	Actual capacity cost vs. planned capacity cost
	Cost of under-provisioning
	Cost of over-provisioning
Processes	Percentage of the IT capacity model that is automated
	Peak demand capacity
	Number of peak demand capacity breaches
	Capacity forecast model coverage of IT resources

Balanced Scorecard Segment	Capability Performance Indicators
Learning and Growth	Number of capacity forecasting incidents caused by non-availability of underlying information
	Fidelity of forecasting data
	Number of capacity forecasting process improvements implemented
Customer	Forecasting assessment coverage of critical business services/operations
	Business user satisfaction with capacity forecast information
	Cost of IT capacity forecasting failures

05: DEMAND AND SUPPLY MANAGEMENT (DSM)

Balanced Scorecard Segment	Capability Performance Indicators
Financial	Cost changes from IT service adjustments
	Business cost of IT service shortfalls
	Savings from retiring IT services
	Savings from replacing IT services
Processes	Accuracy of the forecasted IT service demand
	Speed of response to IT service demand
	Percentage of IT services retired due to lack of demand
Learning and Growth	Percentage of IT services added or expanded as a result of predicted demand
	Number of IT service capacity adjustments
Customer	Percentage of service portfolio adjustments resulting from stakeholder consultation
	Satisfaction with IT services at peak demand

06: ENTERPRISE INFORMATION MANAGEMENT (EIM)

Balanced Scorecard Segment	Capability Performance Indicators
Financial	Costs of information management
	Value of information
	Cost of inaccurate or poor quality data
Processes	Percentage of data that adheres to information standards
	Percentage of data sets that are managed throughout their life cycles
	Percentage of information repositories that use metadata
	Number of access rights modifications for critical IT systems
	Percentage of information repositories that contain duplicate information
Learning and Growth	Usage of data innovation portals
	Number of business intelligence and analysis goals enabled by IT services
	Number of key decisions supported by a Decision Support System (DSS)
Customer	Stakeholder satisfaction with information accessibility
	Stakeholder satisfaction with information quality
	Percentage of employees with assigned data information roles and responsibilities

07: GREEN IT (GIT)

Balanced Scorecard Segment	Capability Performance Indicators
Financial	Cost savings from sustainability initiatives
	Percentage of the IT budget allocated to sustainability efforts
	Employee sustainability incentives

Balanced Scorecard Segment	Capability Performance Indicators
Processes	Carbon footprint of the IT function
	Carbon footprint of the organization
	Percentage of IT equipment in conformance with the organization's sustainability policies
	Percentage reduction in the use of hazardous equipment, material, and components by IT
	Power usage effectiveness (PUE)
	Percentage of IT projects that include sustainability criteria
Learning and Growth	Number of employee suggestions for environmental sustainability that were successfully implemented
	Percentage of IT job roles with environmental sustainability requirements
	Compliance with IT sustainability policies and regulations
Customer	Compliance of suppliers and partners with agreed sustainability policies
	Number of sustainability initiatives jointly implemented with stakeholders
	Stakeholder satisfaction with the effectiveness of environmental sustainability
	Impact of sustainability on brand reputation

08: INNOVATION MANAGEMENT (IM)

Balanced Scorecard Segment	Capability Performance Indicators
Financial	Innovation spending
	Impact of innovations on ROI
Processes	Time to market for innovations
	Idea conversion rate
	Number of innovation launches per time period
	Percentage of innovation projects stopped per investment stage

Balanced Scorecard Segment	Capability Performance Indicators
Learning and Growth	Number of patents generated
	Agility of the innovation cycle
	Percentage of employees with active memberships in innovation networks
	Number of opportunities for innovation skills and knowledge building
Customer	Impact of innovation activities on employee productivity
	Stakeholder satisfaction with innovation activities
	Business unit participation in innovation activities

09: IT LEADERSHIP AND GOVERNANCE (ITG)

Balanced Scorecard Segment	Capability Performance Indicators
Financial	IT funding required to fulfil IT's strategic role
	Total cost of IT
	Cost of IT employee incentives allocated to ensure the delivery of value by IT
Processes	Number of violations to IT policies
	Number of major IT decisions that follow an agreed process
	Percentage of key IT decisions with a published responsibility assignment matrix
Learning and Growth	Percentage of IT managers receiving feedback on IT managerial leadership style
	Number of IT employees who can articulate the IT vision
	Average time to turn strategic IT objectives into initiatives
	Central vs. business unit ownership of IT capabilities

Balanced Scorecard Segment	Capability Performance Indicators
Customer	Percentage of IT decisions that include key stakeholders
	Percentage of stakeholders to whom IT governance processes and decisions are communicated
	Percentage of stakeholders who can accurately describe IT governance processes for decision-making
	Stakeholder satisfaction that IT decisions are made using objective criteria
	Percentage of organizational strategic decisions that have active IT management involvement

10: ORGANIZATION DESIGN AND PLANNING (ODP)

Balanced Scorecard Segment	Capability Performance Indicators
Financial	Savings attributed to organizational structure improvement and other change initiatives
Processes	Accuracy of the organizational chart
	Quality of decision-making processes
	Access to IT expertise
	Quality of structural alignment
	Efficiency of the financial decision-making structures
	Span of control
	Percentage of managers with succession plans in place
	Percentage of sub organizations/business units with a charter in place
Learning and Growth	Impact of change on employee retention
	Percentage of requested changes implemented in response to organizational structure issues
	Employee perception of the IT function's structure to support the organization's strategic direction

Balanced Scorecard Segment	Capability Performance Indicators
Customer	Effectiveness of organizational structure supports in working with external parties
	Employee satisfaction with clarity on their roles and responsibilities
	Percentage of IT employees with whom the organization's culture resonates
	Employee engagement and satisfaction with change

11: RISK MANAGEMENT (RM)

Balanced Scorecard Segment	Capability Performance Indicators
Financial	IT risk exposure
	Cost of IT-related risk incidents
	Risk treatment effectiveness – estimation of potential losses avoided as a result of risk treatments
Processes	Percentage of risk scores exceeding the risk tolerance threshold
	Residual risk scores/risk score changes
	Percentage of identified risks that are not treated
	Number of compliance violations regarding risk/security standards or industry regulations
	Number and impact of materialized risk incidents
Learning and Growth	Percentage of employees with risk management certifications
	Percentage of employees who reported risks that exceeded the risk tolerance threshold
Customer	Stakeholder satisfaction with risk treatment effectiveness
	Risk impact on brand reputation
	Risk impact on operations
	Percentage of identified risks that are co-owned/co-shared with business unit stakeholders

12: SERVICE ANALYTICS AND INTELLIGENCE (SAI)

Balanced Scorecard Segment	Capability Performance Indicators
Financial	End-to-end IT service cost per user
	Cost of over and under IT capacity
	End-to-end IT asset utilization
Processes	Number of IT services defined in business terms
	Number of end-to-end IT services with a dedicated service manager
	Number of critical IT systems and infrastructure with business continuity plans
	Percentage of IT services with automated detection and remediation
	Application health scores
Learning and Growth	Number of end-to-end processes covered by enterprise-level scenario modelling
	Service catalogue coverage
	Ratio of IT services offered to users versus IT services internally defined
Customer	Number of business objectives supported by end-to-end IT services
	Stakeholder satisfaction with IT service reviews
	Time lost due to IT service failures
	Throughput gained due to the addition or expansion of IT services

13: SOURCING (SRC)

Balanced Scorecard Segment	Capability Performance Indicators
Financial	Value of business innovations enabled by external IT service providers
	Financial impact of switching IT service providers
	Total spend on outsourced IT services compared to the IT budget
	Savings from outsourcing non-core activities

Balanced Scorecard Segment	Capability Performance Indicators
Processes	Percentage of sourcing initiatives supported by a business case
	Percentage of IT service providers selected using a standardized approach
	Percentage of IT service providers who meet their contract terms and conditions
	Percentage of outsourced IT services that have contingency plans or alternative service providers in place
Learning and Growth	Percentage of IT service provider partnerships that result in business innovations
	Percentage of outsourcing projects where readiness for outsourcing has been assessed
	Diversity/concentration of IT services among external IT suppliers
Customer	Stakeholder satisfaction with outsourcing initiatives
	Number of supply continuity issues

14: STRATEGIC PLANNING (SP)

Balanced Scorecard Segment	Capability Performance Indicators
Financial	Spend on IT strategic projects
	Revenue attributable to new IT-enabled business capabilities driven by strategic planning
Processes	Percentage of IT priorities aligned to critical business priorities
	Effectiveness of the IT strategic plan
	Percentage of programmes in the IT strategic plan for which a business case is developed
	IT strategic plan approval time
Learning and Growth	Agility of the IT strategic planning cycle
	Percentage of IT strategic planning goals dedicated to research and innovation projects
	Percentage of IT strategic planning goals dedicated to training and upskilling

Balanced Scorecard Segment	Capability Performance Indicators
Customer	Percentage of strategic IT goals for which ownership has been jointly assumed by IT and business units
	Stakeholder agreement with the IT strategic plan
	Stakeholder satisfaction with IT strategic planning

15: BUDGET MANAGEMENT (BGM)

Balanced Scorecard Segment	Capability Performance Indicators
Financial	Actual IT spend versus planned IT spend
	Number of IT budget deviations
	IT OpEx budget as a percentage of the organization's OpEx budget
Processes	Adherence to IT budget reviews
	Ratio of the OpEx vs. CapEx budget
	Percentage of IT budget categories assigned to designated accountable managers
	Percentage of the IT budget allocated to unplanned projects
Learning and Growth	Percentage of IT managers with training in budgeting
	Percentage of the IT budget spent on innovation
	Percentage of IT budget deviations where effective corrective action is taken
Customer	Stakeholder satisfaction with consultation on IT budget planning
	Percentage of the IT budget linked to broader strategic objectives
	Percentage of IT budget expenditure approved using IT budget oversight structures

16: BUDGET OVERSIGHT AND PERFORMANCE ANALYSIS (BOP)

Balanced Scorecard Segment	Capability Performance Indicators
Financial	Business value resulting from unit cost adjustments
	Budget oversight performance cost savings
	Expenditure rate
	Year-on-year percentage change in IT budget allocations by category
Processes	Percentage of budget categories that have budget metrics reported
	Percentage of IT projects and operations activities with budget tracking and trending analysis
	Percentage of IT budget categories with multi-year forecasting
	Percentage of budget performance analysis activities that are automated
Learning and Growth	Percentage of IT projects' budget corrective actions that are implemented
	Timeliness of IT budget data availability
	Percentage alignment of IT budget practices and terminology with those standardized across the organization
Customer	Percentage of the IT budget directly aligned to business objectives
	Stakeholder satisfaction with IT budget oversight
	Frequency of communication on budget performance to stakeholders

17: FUNDING AND FINANCING (FF)

Balanced Scorecard Segment	Capability Performance Indicators
Financial	Ratio of internal to external IT funding sources
	Change in total IT funding as a percentage of the organization's revenue
	Cost of IT financing

Balanced Scorecard Segment	Capability Performance Indicators
Processes	Percentage breakdown of funding by categories of IT activity
	Number of funding sources reviews completed
	Percentage of funding decisions that occur in alignment with an agreed funding governance model
Learning and Growth	Competitive benchmark of IT innovation funding
	Competitive benchmark of IT funding sources
	Percentage of senior stakeholders who understand IT funding options
	Percentage growth in the identified sources of funding available
Customer	Return on investment (ROI) in IT
	Percentage of overall IT funding aligned to specific business strategic priorities/ objectives
	Transparency of IT funding decisions to stakeholders

18: PORTFOLIO PLANNING AND PRIORITIZATION (PPP)

Balanced Scorecard Segment	Capability Performance Indicators
Financial	Planned vs. actual portfolio spend
	Ratio of portfolio over-spend to portfolio under-spend
	Spend on strategic programmes and projects
	Spend per portfolio category
Processes	Percentage of programmes and projects that use an investment evaluation framework for selection and prioritization
	Resource level availability vs. shortfall
Learning and Growth	Percentage of programmes and projects that have recurring resource issues
	Programme and project delivery accuracy

Balanced Scorecard Segment	Capability Performance Indicators
Customer	Percentage of programmes and projects with appropriate sign-off
	Percentage of key stakeholders involved in portfolio selection and prioritization
	Percentage of programmes and projects that are delivered compared to active programmes and projects in the portfolio
	Stakeholder satisfaction with the alignment of the portfolio with the IT strategy

19: CAPABILITY ASSESSMENT MANAGEMENT (CAM)

Balanced Scorecard Segment	Capability Performance Indicators
Financial	IT capability improvement funding
	Cost savings achieved by IT capability improvements
	Value of rewards allocated for employees' contributions to IT capability improvements
	IT capability improvements for which funding is not available
Processes	Number of IT capability assessments that use the same evaluation framework
	Number of IT capability assessments that are completed
	Percentage of IT capability improvement targets that are achieved
Learning and Growth	Employee awareness of IT capability assessment and improvement activities
	Percentage of IT capability targets informed by industry benchmarks
Customer	Percentage of IT capability improvement initiatives with senior stakeholder sponsorship
	Number of IT capability gaps, that have assigned personnel, who are responsible for their resolution
	Stakeholder satisfaction levels with IT capability improvement initiatives
	Percentage of IT capability improvement initiatives with successful outcomes

20: ENTERPRISE ARCHITECTURE MANAGEMENT (EAM)

Balanced Scorecard Segment	Capability Performance Indicators
Financial	Percentage reduction in IT development costs
	Percentage of revenue that is processed through standard platforms
	Enterprise architecture cost savings
Processes	Percentage of projects that are compliant with enterprise architectural standards
	Percentage of projects with assigned enterprise architects
	Percentage of IT services that use a standard platform
	Number of deviations from agreed enterprise architecture principles
	Number of enterprise architecture domains with up-to-date roadmaps
Learning and Growth	Percentage of enterprise architects with defined career paths
	Number of innovative ideas implemented
Customer	Percentage of enterprise architecture plans approved by relevant stakeholders
	Percentage of projects that deliver solutions based on the approved enterprise architecture
	Percentage of business units with enterprise architecture roadmaps
	Enterprise architecture approval ratings

21: INFORMATION SECURITY MANAGEMENT (ISM)

Balanced Scorecard Segment	Capability Performance Indicators
Financial	IT spend on information security
	Cost of information security-related incidents
	Information security risk exposure

Balanced Scorecard Segment	Capability Performance Indicators
Processes	Number of information security incidents
	Percentage of information security breaches addressed
	Average time to restore availability of high-priority systems
	Percentage of new projects/initiatives that receive an information security compliance sign-off
	Information security audits – comparison of issues per time period
	Time to close an information security incident
	Number of compliance violations with data security classifications
Learning and Growth	Percentage of employees with information security-related certifications
Customer	Stakeholder satisfaction with information security management effectiveness
	Information security incident impact on brand
	Information security incident impact on operations

22: KNOWLEDGE ASSET MANAGEMENT (KAM)

Balanced Scorecard Segment	Capability Performance Indicators
Financial	Revenue generated from patents
Processes	Percentage of business functions whose knowledge needs are documented
	Percentage of employees who use the knowledge repository
	Percentage of employees who use specialist knowledge tools
	Average knowledge request response time
Learning and Growth	Number of subscriptions to knowledge services
	Time provided for knowledge management activities
	Percentage of employees who participate in knowledge/expert communities
	Number of interactive knowledge sharing events within the organization
	Percentage of annual reviews that mention knowledge management

Balanced Scorecard Segment	Capability Performance Indicators
Customer	Employee satisfaction with knowledge acquisition
	Employee satisfaction with knowledge sharing
	Employee satisfaction with the speed of communicating new knowledge

23: PEOPLE ASSET MANAGEMENT (PAM)

Balanced Scorecard Segment	Capability Performance Indicators
Financial	IT contractor headcount costs
	IT headcount costs
Processes	Time to job acceptance
	Number of job offers accepted
	Average number of job applicants meeting job specification requirements
	Number of IT employees whose jobs were terminated involuntarily
	Percentage of employees satisfactorily performing job duties and responsibilities
	Percentage of job roles where skill gaps have been quantified
Learning and Growth	Percentage of employees who have had performance appraisals conducted
	Percentage of IT employees who have completed developmental assignments
	Percentage of IT employees who have mentors
	Percentage of managerial positions that have "ready" candidates identified for potential succession
	Average percentage of employee development goals met across all employees
Customer	Managers' satisfaction with new hire performance
	Employee job satisfaction
	Employee absentee rate
	IT employee turnover
	IT employee tenure

24: PERSONAL DATA PROTECTION (PDP)

Balanced Scorecard Segment	Capability Performance Indicators
Financial	Cost to resolve data protection incidents
	Cost of the data protection service
Processes	Number of data protection breaches
	Percentage of IT projects that have data protection impact assessments conducted
	Percentage of personal data with documented justification for its use
	Percentage of personal data with documented consent
Learning and Growth	Percentage of employees with data protection training
	Percentage of potential data protection issues that were identified, and avoided or mitigated
Customer	Number of data protection issues successfully resolved
	Stakeholder satisfaction with the organization's data protection function
	Percentage of employees who are aware of their responsibilities for protecting personal data
	Percentage data protection compliance with data protection legislation and statutory requirements

25: PROGRAMME AND PROJECT MANAGEMENT (PPM)

Balanced Scorecard Segment	Capability Performance Indicators
Financial	Number of IT programmes and projects that are within budget
	Cost Variance (CV) of all IT programmes and projects
	ROI for IT programmes and projects

Balanced Scorecard Segment	Capability Performance Indicators
Processes	Schedule Performance Index (SPI)
	Number of programme and project missed milestones
	Number of programmes and projects using agreed methodologies
	Percentage of programmes and projects that follow a standardized risk management process
	Percentage of programmes and projects that follow an agreed change management process
Learning and Growth	Percentage of programme and project roles with defined responsibilities and accountabilities
	Number of learnings captured from completed programmes and projects
Customer	Stakeholder satisfaction with programme and project status reporting
	Project success rates
	Average project cycle time/duration

26: RELATIONSHIP MANAGEMENT (REM)

Balanced Scorecard Segment	Capability Performance Indicators
Financial	Cost savings due to resolution of business problems by technical solutions
	Number of jointly sponsored IT–business projects
Processes	Coverage of relationships with an account/business relationship manager
	Percentage of IT-related issues for which consultation takes place with stakeholders
	Percentage of jointly sponsored IT–business projects that result in business innovations
Learning and Growth	Percentage of top-level organizational executive meetings that include the CIO
	Stakeholder perception of the alignment of IT services with business priorities
	Percentage of service portfolio updates that are driven by users

Balanced Scorecard Segment	Capability Performance Indicators
Customer	Business unit satisfaction with the service delivered by the IT function
	End-user satisfaction with the service delivered by the IT function
	Stakeholder satisfaction with the quality of IT-related communications across the organization

27: RESEARCH, DEVELOPMENT AND ENGINEERING (RDE)

Balanced Scorecard Segment	Capability Performance Indicators
Financial	Impact of technology research work on ROI
	Percentage of the IT budget dedicated to IT RDE
	Percentage of the IT RDE budget co-funded by other business units
	Percentage of the IT RDE budget sourced from external funding sources
Processes	RDE ideation – Ratio of ideas generated to ideas transferred to other departments for deeper evaluation
	Percentage of technology research outputs resulting in successful pilots
	Percentage of technology research projects stopped at each investment stage
	Percentage of new product or service launches originating from technology research activities
Learning and Growth	Number of books or whitepapers published
	Number of peer-reviewed publications
	Number of patents generated
	Percentage of employees who are aware of approaches for identifying and evaluating new technologies
	Percentage of RDE employees participating in conferences

Balanced Scorecard Segment	Capability Performance Indicators
Customer	Percentage of other business units participating in technology research programmes
	Impact of technology research activities on employee productivity
	Customer satisfaction with new products or services arising from technology research activities

28: SERVICE PROVISIONING (SRP)

Balanced Scorecard Segment	Capability Performance Indicators
Financial	Cost of IT service outages
	Cost of corrective actions required to meet service levels
	Cost savings from the reduction in problem-related incidents
	Average cost per call/contact
Processes	Percentage of IT services with a service level agreement
	Average incident turnaround time
	Number of IT incidents
	Number of IT problems per time period
	Mean time to repair a configuration item or an IT service
	Percentage of IT service releases that are automated
	First time fix rate
	First level (support) fixes
	Percentage of IT services documented in the IT services catalogue
	Mean time between failures
Learning and Growth	Percentage of changes successfully deployed
	Number of unplanned/emergency changes
	Number of IT service changes that require roll-backs

Balanced Scorecard Segment	Capability Performance Indicators
Customer	Availability of IT services (uptime)
	Call abandon rate
	Percentage of IT services that satisfy their service level agreements
	Number of customer complaints related to the quality of IT service levels

29: SOLUTIONS DELIVERY (SD)

Balanced Scorecard Segment	Capability Performance Indicators
Financial	Cost variance for IT solutions
	Cost per function point
	IT solutions delivery costs vs. savings
	IT solutions delivery costs vs. revenue
	Cost of poor application performance
Processes	Planned vs. actual IT solutions delivery schedule
	Percentage of IT solutions delivered in accordance with a test strategy
	Percentage of IT solutions that use release management
	Percentage of IT solutions that use configuration management
	Percentage of delivered IT solutions that use agreed standards, methods, and tools
Learning and Growth	Time spent on correcting IT solutions defects
	Percentage of requirements delivered by IT solutions
Customer	End user satisfaction with IT solutions delivery
	Time to deliver IT solutions
	Percentage of approved requests for IT solutions that are overdue

30: SUPPLIER MANAGEMENT (SUM)

Balanced Scorecard Segment	Capability Performance Indicators
Financial	Cost of IT supplier management
	Cost of switching suppliers
	Spend per segmented supply base
Processes	Percentage of IT suppliers that meet agreed performance objectives
	Percentage of IT suppliers with quality ratings
	Percentage of IT suppliers with regular performance reviews
Learning and Growth	Number of innovations arising from supplier collaboration
	Employee participation in professional networks pertaining to supplier management
	Percentage of improvements made to the supplier management process
Customer	Percentage of suppliers with assigned relationship/account managers
	Business unit satisfaction with IT suppliers
	Stakeholder satisfaction with ongoing business alignment

31: TECHNICAL INFRASTRUCTURE MANAGEMENT (TIM)

Balanced Scorecard Segment	Capability Performance Indicators
Financial	CapEx to OpEx ratio
	Infrastructure cost per user
	IT infrastructure maintenance costs
	Percentage of technology assets in use beyond their depreciation schedules
	IT infrastructure variable vs. fixed costs

Balanced Scorecard Segment	Capability Performance Indicators
Processes	System uptime
	Utilization rates for the IT infrastructure
	Percentage of the IT infrastructure that is managed via a configuration management database
	Percentage of the IT infrastructure that is covered by a service level agreement
	Rate of IT infrastructure compliance with service level agreements
	Recovery time objective
	Percentage of the IT infrastructure that is virtualized
	Percentage of the IT infrastructure that is automatically managed
	Server to system administrator ratio
Learning and Growth	Percentage of successful improvements implemented to the IT infrastructure
	Forecast accuracy of IT infrastructure provisioning
	IT infrastructure unavailability
Customer	Stakeholder satisfaction with the IT infrastructure
	Average time for IT infrastructure hardware provisioning

32: USER EXPERIENCE DESIGN (UED)

Balanced Scorecard Segment	Capability Performance Indicators
Financial	Change in employee productivity from UX-enabled improvements to IT products or services
	User support costs
	Impact on ROI arising from innovations or improvements that result from UX activities

Balanced Scorecard Segment	Capability Performance Indicators
Processes	Percentage of users involved in the design process
	Percentage of IT projects with UX activities built into their project plans
	Percentage of users who can perform a core set of tasks using IT products or services with no help as a result of UX activities
	Number of user touchpoints taken into consideration in the wider UX planning and design processes
Learning and Growth	Percentage of targeted IT development employees with UX training
	Percentage of UX employees attending user experience research or design-related conferences
	Percentage of ideas incorporated into IT products or services arising from UX activities
	Number of UX design process enhancements
Customer	Percentage of IT products or services that have completed a usability evaluation
	User satisfaction with the ease of use of IT products or services
	Customer satisfaction with the user experience of new IT products or services

33: USER TRAINING MANAGEMENT (UTM)

Balanced Scorecard Segment	Capability Performance Indicators
Financial	Training budget allocation
	Impact of training on user support costs
	Impact of training on employee productivity
Processes	Percentage of targeted employees trained
	Cost per training method
	Percentage of employees that undergo proficiency levels assessments
Learning and Growth	Employee competence levels
	Percentage of training courses related to innovation
	Frequency of training course refresh cycles

Balanced Scorecard Segment	Capability Performance Indicators
Customer	Employee satisfaction with training
	Percentage uptake of training courses
	Effectiveness of training

34: BENEFITS ASSESSMENT AND REALIZATION (BAR)

Balanced Scorecard Segment	Capability Performance Indicators
Financial	Business value of IT-enabled change initiatives
	IT business case – forecasted vs. actual value delivered
Processes	Number of investments that use a benefits plan
	Number of investments that use the standard business case process
	Percentage of change programmes that use the standardized governance framework
Learning and Growth	Percentage of stakeholders trained in behavioural change
	Percentage of managers trained in benefits assessment and realization
	Percentage of IT-enabled change initiatives that include a 'lessons learned' review
Customer	Business sponsor satisfaction ratings with benefits realization
	End-user satisfaction ratings with benefits delivered
	Cycle time to realize benefits from new or enhanced services
	Stakeholder engagement in benefits realization programmes

35: PORTFOLIO MANAGEMENT (PM)

Balanced Scorecard Segment	Capability Performance Indicators
Financial	Value creation from IT-enabled programmes
	Financial resource monitoring of the portfolio
Processes	IT portfolio status
	Number of programmes and projects that are in compliance with the organization's portfolio standards
Learning and Growth	Percentage of programmes and projects that use value-at-risk analysis
	Percentage of programmes and projects that use scenario analysis
	Number of corrective actions required to maintain the programme objectives
	Number of missed portfolio outcomes/forecasts
Customer	Percentage of programmes and projects with sponsors who are actively engaged
	Stakeholder satisfaction with the business value delivered by the IT portfolio
	Percentage of the portfolio that uses benefits tracking

36: TOTAL COST OF OWNERSHP (TCO)

Balanced Scorecard Segment	Capability Performance Indicators
Financial	TCO of IT services year on year
	TCO of IT assets year on year
	Percentage of TCO savings targets realized
	Percentage of year on year cost reductions per IT service
Processes	Percentage of IT assets and services whose TCO is tracked
	Frequency of TCO model review
	Refresh rate of TCO data

Balanced Scorecard Segment	Capability Performance Indicators
Learning and Growth	Percentage of strategic IT portfolio/investment decisions supported by TCO data
	TCO of IT services vs. external benchmarks
	TCO of IT assets vs. external benchmarks
Customer	Percentage of managers who are trained in the full life cycle costs of IT
	TCO forecast accuracy
	Percentage of business ecosystem partners with linkages to TCO data

Sample Artefacts 4

Artefacts are tools, templates, and information developed and tested by IVI and IVI consortium members on real world projects. They are important and helpful in the implementation of capability improvement in an organization. The following table presents a small representative sample of the artefacts that are available to IVI partners and licensed users.

Artefact	Description
CIP User Guide	Describes how to set up and manage an IT Capability Improvement Programme. (.pdf)
Guide to Assessment Selection	Guides users in selecting the most appropriate initial assessment. (.pdf)
CIP Roadmap Template	A template programme plan that includes all key milestones and activities. (.xls)
CIP Team Role Matrix	A template to understand, identify, and record all key programme participants. (.xls)
CIP SOW Template	A template programme/project statement of work for a capability improvement. (.doc)
CIP Workshop Guides	A detailed guide to running each of the four key workshops in the CIP life cycle. (.doc)
Benefits Planning Template	A template for target CIP benefits to be defined and documented. (.doc)
Benefits Register Template	A template record to track, monitor, and share benefits realized. (.xls)
CPI Template	A form for calculation and presentation of over 400 key capability performance indicators. (.doc)
Analysis Worksheet	A sophisticated .xls workbook for assessment, data analysis, and presentation. (.xls)

Artefact	Description
Template Assessment Report	A template report for the presentation of IT-CMF assessment findings. (.doc)

The artefacts represent a small selection of the resources available to licensed users of IT-CMF. There is also a 'partner pack', which is an additional set of artefacts for approved and certified IVI partners – included in this pack are the tools and resources to promote and deliver IT-CMF based business solutions for the partner's end customers.

Access to the IVI body of knowledge, e-learning, assessments, and all artefacts is via the IVI member and user portal – www.ivi.ie/portal.